'Twas Seeding Time

'Twas Seeding Time

John L. Ruth

A Mennonite View of the
American Revolution

HERALD PRESS
Scottdale, Pennsylvania
Kitchener, Ontario

'TWAS SEEDING TIME
Copyright©1976 by John L. Ruth
Published by Herald Press, Scottdale, Pa. 15683
    Released simultaneously in Canada by Herald Press,
    Kitchener, Ontario N2G 4M5
Library of Congress Catalog Card Number: 76-41475
International Standard Book Number: 0-8361-1800-6
Printed in the United States of America
Design: Alice B. Shetler

Contents

Author's Preface

This book is a footnote to American Revolutionary history. It deals with material that has been considered unimportant or marginal by historians of the Revolution (a recent two-volume history does not even mention an encampment to which I give four or five pages), and it seeks to assign center stage, for a moment, to facts that are usually lost in the tumult of the times. This is a distorting of perspective—but then, conventional perspectives on the Revolution have been so overwhelmingly the rule that an alternative may be found suggestive.

I had not wished to write even so informal a history as this, but would have preferred to reflect on history as written by others, and then to compose, in an artistic attempt, a story to illustrate and interpret attitudes of people who for reasons of their Christian faith refrained from cooperating in the Revolution. Only because there existed no history of Mennonite experience in these times did I presume to draw up, in some haste, a brief connected narrative based on such literal facts as I could collect in a few months with the aid of several valued friends. I have wondered, from time to time, how a people like the Mennonites, supposedly preoccupied with their past, have for so long maintained only a rudimentary knowledge of their forebears' colonial American experience.

There has been no attempt to hide the fact that I am

not an uninterested spectator of the events I describe. I have been investigating the sources of traditions in the midst of which I was nurtured. I have written most of these words within two miles of Funk's mill, as the crow flies, and have driven daily by the farms of my "characters" Christian Moyer and Henry Rosenberger. They, with Bishop Christian Funk, are· my ancestors seven or eight generations back. I have sought not to inflate the significance of their acts, nor to gloss over the pettiness of their squabbles. I have stuck to documentable data. I have tried to learn, more than to celebrate, though I have allowed myself, in a closing "Fantasy," a lyric mood.

The records I have found, or which have been graciously shared with me by Robert F. Ulle and S. Duane Kauffman, have been, by ordinary standards, often tangential and minor. I was not weighed down by bulk. Ironically, our distorting access to the personal lives of the Franconia Mennonite ministers of the era hangs largely on the embittered account of a lengthy quarrel among them, caused by the stresses of the times. Readers with scholarly interests, however, will be able to consult considerable further material in the forthcoming important "source book" described in my closing "Note."

I owe hearty thanks to Robert F. Ulle, whose freely shared and extremely valuable research was crucial to my narrative. Likewise, Duane Kauffman discovered and made available to me previously forgotten or unknown materials. The Eastern Pennsylvania Mennonite Historical Library, located at the Christopher Dock High School near Lansdale, Pennsylvania, was the base point of my search, and bore patiently with my months-long abuse of my privileges there. The work of Wilmer Reinford, in collecting and preserving its materials, has only begun to bear fruit such as this story.

Thanks are due to my old friends Abram and Grace Landis, who made it possible for me to find a quiet place to begin my writing, in their woodland cabin.

'Twas Seeding Time is the product solely of the support and encouragement of the Franconia Mennonite community, and two books which I finished just previously were likewise enhanced far beyond what would have been possible had I not been able to lean heavily on the "Heritage Council" created for my support and guidance. I cannot refrain from expressing my happiness here in response to the truly rare spirit of concern of my "Franconia" spiritual community that its members' gifts be cherished and shared with those beyond its own geographic borders. I say this with no sense of having been "controlled" by the community which sought to enable me.

In particular I should like to mention the names of R. Wayne Clemens, chiefly instrumental in conceiving and setting up the Heritage Council, and those who have served on it: John Fretz, Robert Landis, Hiram Hershey, Alice Rittenhouse, Gerald Studer, Gerald Weaver, and the exceptionally understanding chairman, Walton Hackman. To them and to many other local Mennonites who have made it possible for me to gather stories that speak of and to our life as a covenant people, my heartfelt thanks.

John L. Ruth
Harleysville, Pennsylvania
June 22, 1976

Chapter 1

Defenseless Christians and Bloody Tomahawks

On the final day of 1755 a train of seven heavily loaded wagons could be seen rolling northward from the Pennsylvania Mennonite communities of Skippack and Franconia. A melancholy emergency was the cause of this unseasonal expedition which marked the end of an era of good feeling. Angry Indians had crossed the long Blue Mountain to where the white men's smoke curled peacefully from recently built hearths, and left behind in the ashes of their cabins the smoldering, scalpless bodies of European settlers. Now over 500 stunned refugees had huddled into the Moravian settlements of Bethlehem and Nazareth, and a plea had gone out for relief.

Although the situation was new for Pennsylvanians, the Mennonites had a centuries-old memory of dealing with the needs of homeless people, and men appointed to oversee any such work: deacons. Christian Meyer and Valentine Hunsicker had promptly collected from their congregations at Franconia, Salford, and Skippack tons of meal, eighty-five bushels of grain, twelve bushels of apple

"schnitz," and supplies of meat, butter, and salt. From
the looms of several families had come thirteen yards of
linen, and someone donated four pairs of children's shoes.
"Four ounces of thread," spun in Perkiomen Township,
was perhaps meant to mend clothes torn in terrified flight
from the Indians. A practical people, these transported
German-speaking farmers were slow of tongue but quick
to lend a hand to people in trouble.

Deacon Christian Meyer, now in his early fifties, kept a
careful book on his family's financial dealings, as well as
one for the "alms" of the local Mennonite meetings. He
had a young niece, Esther Funk, who, "lame in all her
limbs," depended for her food, lodging, and even wash-
ing on the goodness of her family. His own brother,
Jacob, was likewise incompetent. Although the Meyers
and Funks, well-to-do as farmers and millers, were eco-
nomically able to support their weak members, there
were others in this community settled only three decades
earlier who were dependent on the church. There was, as
yet, no government or public provision for the poor or
weak. As treasurer of the alms fund, Deacon Meyer
therefore received in trust anywhere from several shillings to ten pounds whenever the will of a local Mennonite
farmer was executed.

His sister's husband, miller and Bishop Henry Funk,
had not yet written a will, but had recently recognized the
approach of old age by ordaining his own son, Christian,
as a minister in the local congregation, Indianfield, at the
log meetinghouse standing on land taken from the edge
of Deacon Meyer's farm. The ordination had occurred in
the very months of the Indian troubles in Northampton
County, a day's journey to the north. The new minister,

in his mid-twenties, was clearly cut out for leadership, inheriting the mantle of his influential father, Henry, the largest landholder of the community, first miller along the Indian Creek, and the first Mennonite author in America. Bishop Henry's four oldest children, before the birth of lame Esther, had been sons. The oldest, John, was an established blacksmith in the newer community of Hilltown just to the northeast, and Abraham, the youngest, was being groomed for the home mill. Christian, the new minister, would receive the home farm, except for the mill.

Having settled in the wilderness north of Philadelphia three decades earlier, the Funk and Meyer families had lived through a war-scare in the 1740s, but this was the first time that there had been casualties. The earlier tensions had spurred Henry Funk to write a letter, with several of his fellow ministers, to the Mennonites of Holland. It asked for assistance in publishing a translation for the young Mennonites of Pennsylvania of a massive Dutch book of inspirational stories entitled the *Martyrs Mirror*. Though the Dutch Mennonites had, in past years, helped many a Swiss or Palatine family to pay their passage across the Atlantic, they themselves were now far past the age of persecution, and they had little enthusiasm for this project. Instead, Bishop Funk had the joy of observing the huge task taken over by a Sabbatarian Dunkard monastery at Ephrata, sixty miles west of Indian Creek, and just north of the Swiss Mennonite settlements of Lancaster County. Having carefully proofread, with nearby Minister Dielman Kolb of Salford, every page of the new edition as it came from the press, Henry Funk was able to recommend the book to his young people on its appearance in 1751. It was meant to teach them from the history of their Mennonite forebears in Europe that the way of the cross might demand heroism.

Henry had written a book himself, published in Germantown by the new German printer, Christopher Saur, in 1744. Only a mile down the Indian Creek from his mill was the home of John Price, a Dunkard minister, whose fellow believers met on his farm and immersed their new members in the nearby creek. Bishop Funk's little volume, *A Mirror of Baptism*, had been directed against both the Dunkard requirement of immersion and the Quaker insistence that "baptism by Holy Ghost" was enough, without an outward sign. Now he had a larger book of his mind.

A new generation was, after all, at hand, and they needed teaching lest they forget the very issues of freedom of conscience for which their parents had left Alpine farms and Palatine *Hofs*. The sainted William Penn had proclaimed a land of jubilee across the ocean, where jealous neighbors would be prevented, by original charter, from harassing the defenseless, nonpolitical Anabaptists. No social penalty was to be paid, in this wilderness of great freedom, for one's non-affiliation with a state-church. And so they had come, with Welsh Quakers, German Lutherans, Swiss Reformed, Moravians, Schwenkfelders, Dunkards, and their own Amish relatives. First hesitantly, and then in a rush, some three thousand Mennonites had already found peace in Pennsylvania.

There had been no real trouble with the Indians on the land the Mennonites bought. Penn had "paid" their chiefs, or "sachems," as they called them, by various gifts, trifling to the white man, but redolent of brotherly affection to the Indians. Most of them had now moved north and west of the Blue Mountain which arched from the Lehigh River southwest across the Susquehanna. The friendly red folk who did not emigrate traded with the white man and came to his communal frolics. On the farm sloping east from Christian Meyer's, the Henry Clemmer family observed the yearly visit of an Indian to the grave of a former Indian chief, solemnized by the placing of a tobacco leaf on the hallowed spot. After the Indian had gone, the Clemmers' hired man would put the leaf in his pipe and smoke it. Along the Saucon Creek, not far south of Bethlehem, the Yoder, Geissinger, and Landis families had been regularly joined in their Sunday meetings by a group of local Delawares. Along Tohickon Creek, in the easternmost settlement of the Mennonites, immigrant Christian Fretz did have his horse stolen by Indians, but he followed them and rode it home after they had shown they were about to retire by shouting into the woods to scare off lurking animals. Between Salford and Skippack several squaws, left behind when their Delaware relatives trekked westward, tended the cattle of Minister Jacob Shoemaker and did other chores, receiving in return food and lodging and finally a place for their bones on the neighboring farm of the Mennonite Lederachs.

In the Lancaster settlements to the west it was much the same story. There the Mennonite children played with their red counterparts, racing and wrestling while the chiefs watched gleefully. One of the Indian boys, Christy, had been named for someone in the settlement of Hersheys, Brubakers, and Herrs at Conestoga, and he

taught the white boys how to make bows and arrows.
When the Mennonite settlements had filled up, and the
second generation of the Bowman family looked for new
farmland, an Indian offered to show Jacob Bowman good
hunting ground to the north. Although tension had
begun to be felt as Scotch-Irish squatters began to push
beyond lands covered by treaty, Jacob decided, against
his neighbors' advice, to trust the Indian. His red friend
helped him to lay out 300 acres along Muddy Creek, but
observed that there was no good luck in living beside
water that ran toward the sunset, as did the Conestoga.
He invited Jacob to follow him over an Indian trail
through a small range of hills northward to a creek that
ran east, through Berks County, into the Schuylkill River.
The Indian's own home was by the banks of this clear
stream, and he helped Jacob build a cabin a mile and a
half south of this site. "Friend Jacob," said the native
American, "tell your white friends that you have found a
friend who is a friend indeed."

But by the 1750s the Delaware Indians' trust of the
white man had gone sour. William Penn had long gone
the way of all flesh, and his sons and their agents were
motivated by commercial interests. Had even this been
the sole problem, much could have been done to mollify
the Indians by benevolent Quakers. But far over the
heads of the Mennonite farmers of Pennsylvania was
gathering a tidal storm—the clash of French and English
empire-builders. The American phase of this worldwide
struggle brought French fur-traders down from the Great
Lakes to build strings of forts by which they hoped to
block the westward expansion of Pennsylvania and Virginia. If they could establish their hold down across the

continent to Louisiana there would be a French as well as an English America. The stakes were enormous and the clash, by human standards, unavoidable.

The French, who were freer to live among the Indians and even intermarry with them, gained their military alliance. When war was declared in May of 1756, the French incited them to bloody raids along the Pennsylvania frontiers. In these border areas the Indians had in the past decade grown first indignant and then outraged to see Scotch-Irish squatters spilling across the Blue Mountain seeking land, in spite of the agreements with William Penn which had kept the white man south and east of the Appalachians. Working on the roof of his house on the west side of the Lehigh River, Ulrich Showalter, one of the northernmost Mennonites of Pennsylvania, saw a dozen Indians wading toward what he did not realize until later was the butchery of several neighboring families. From Harrisburg to Easton frontier families fled to fortresses and towns, or risked sudden massacre.

One Amish family, Jacob Hochstetlers who lived within two miles of Blue Mountain, elected to stay on their farm, unsuspecting that they might be the special mark of Indian grudging. On a moonless September night in 1757, after an apple schnitzing frolic which had lasted until the morning hours, the Hochstetler's dog awakened Jacob, Jr. When the young man opened the door to see what might have disturbed the dog, he was greeted by a gunshot in his leg. He slammed the door shut and locked it while the family sprang from their beds. Out near the bakehouse eight or ten Indians could be seen in consultation.

Two other sons, Joseph and Christian, known to be excellent marksmen, seized their trusty guns, but their
Swiss Amish father forbade them to fire at the Indians.
They begged him to change his doctrine in this
emergency, but he had not come all the way to America
to give up what he had been taught at home. Then the Indians set fire to the house and withdrew. The family beat
back the fire desperately, and wet it down with their new-
made cider. Finally, unable to bear the heat, they
squirmed out through a ground-level window. Mrs.
Hochstetler was too fat to get through easily, and Jacob,
with his mangled leg, had to be helped. Joseph immediately dashed away and outran the Indians, but the
rest of the family were captured, as the Indians had surrounded them by the time they were out.

The wounded Jacob, Jr., and his sister were tomahawked on the spot, and the mother as well, after
having been stabbed in the heart with particular malice.
Father Jacob and son Christian were led away captive,
along with Joseph, who had been hiding behind a log
nearby, not realizing that the Indians had observed him
crouching down. He was always to claim, in after years,
that the whole family could have been saved, had his
father allowed the sons the use of their guns. It would be
six years before they escaped or were returned under the
terms of a treaty.

From Virginia came a similar dreary tale, where in the
following May one Mennonite family was entirely killed
off by the Indians, and thirty-one Mennonite families
made homeless. Benjamin Hershey, a minister from near
Lancaster town in Pennsylvania, wrote a letter for two of
their men to take to Holland, once more to ask for fi-

nancial aid for dispossessed Mennonites.

No one was more troubled by such events than the Quakers, who up to this point had controlled the Pennsylvania legislature, called the Assembly, and made only token allowance for the organization of military forces to meet this chaos. Among their most conscientious Philadelphia members was the wealthy merchant Israel Pemberton. With fellow Friends he now organized a "Friendly Association" by which, it was hoped, a renewed state of respect could be gained between Indians and their Pennsylvania neighbors. They appealed to other nonresistant groups, such as the Mennonites and Schwenkfelders, for aid in building up a fund from which "presents" could be purchased for meetings with the aggrieved Indians. They felt, according to those who disagreed with their motives, that "the Indian War arose on account of the unjust treatment of the Indians, and was carried on under unholy purposes." This enraged the Scotch-Irish frontier dwellers, who were developing into a political party which the Quakers called "Presbyterians." What the Scotch-Irish found intolerable was that the Quaker-dominated Assembly, supported by Mennonite votes as well as those of other nonresistant groups who lived in the tranquil interior, would not legislate military measures for the protection of those who lived where the danger was.

Although only one fifth of the total population was Quaker, two thirds of the Assembly seats were won by Quakers in the election of October 1755. It was a hot contest, with Brethren editor Saur calling out an enormous German vote on the Quaker side. It was of course impossible for the devout Quakers who believed

that nonviolence was of the essence of the Christian faith
to place ammunition in the hands of their neighbors. As a
result, a confrontation developed between Quakers and
those in the Pennsylvania government who demanded
that a militia be organized, and the Quakers were forced
to begin to withdraw somewhat from their dominant
political role in Penn's Holy Experiment. Still, they voted
and campaigned, and bitter feelings toward them flourished along the Susquehanna frontier.

The Mennonites of Franconia and Skippack kept close
contact with the Friendly Association, through minister
Andrew Ziegler, a vigorous saddler and shoemaker, and
son-in-law of Dielman Kolb, who had helped to proofread
the new translation of the *Martyrs Mirror*. Andrew was
a forceful if opinionated leader, often called upon to witness deeds or wills in the neighborhood, as he did for the
elderly schoolteacher Christopher Dock, instructor of
Andrew's sons at the nearby Salford meetinghouse-
school. Christopher referred to Andrew as an "honest
man." The saddler-preacher could write and speak a
Quakerly if crudely pronounced English. He helped to
raise a contribution of some 400 pounds to the Friendly
Association among the Mennonites. The Mennonite
contact in Lancaster was the elderly Benjamin Hershey,
who reported that about half of his people were ready to
subscribe, but that some were not willing because they
had been "persuaded by some people of other societys
not to do anything towards any such thing, but if they had
anything to spare to give it to the poor." But, in the midst
of reports of Indian atrocities, it was an unpopular suggestion to the military-minded Pennsylvania neighbors of
the Mennonites that Indians should be given presents.

One influential man in Philadelphia who took a dim view of both Christian nonresistance and German-speaking Pennsylvanians was the politician Benjamin Franklin. He had risked his own money to raise a militia and supply the ill-fated British General Braddock with wagons. "This will in a few years," he had once written to a friend, "become a German colony; Instead of their Learning our Language, we must learn theirs, or live as in a foreign Country." He complained that the Germans who came to Pennsylvania were ignorant and illiterate (though he noted at the same time that they printed many books), and he especially resented the opinion-molding effectiveness of the newspaper Christopher Saur published in Germantown. Franklin tried to issue a rival paper in German, but it failed. Though he prided himself on being "a leather-apron man," he could not appreciate the Germanic country style. "The Dutch under-live, and are thereby enabled to under-work and under-sell the English," he remarked, "who are thereby extreamly incommoded, and consequently disgusted." It was, of course, possible for an Englishman to take a more positive view, such as that of a Welsh Quaker who wrote at about the same time, "It is pretty to behold our back settlements, where the barns are large as palaces, while the owners live in log huts; a sign, though, of thriving farms."

It was true, by their own confession, that the Mennonites were "not Exquisite in the English Language." Andrew Ziegler, whose minister-father had not been able to sign his own name, wrote to the Quakers of a meeting he had held "Do-day," and Christopher Dock described his plantation as "blessed with good water and good meddowe." The Lancaster Mennonites, of pure Swiss origin, were even more limited in their English than the Skippack settlement, which had a strong blend of Dutch-speaking people with names like Gaedtschalck, Keyser, Rittenhouse, and Tyson. In the military excitement of 1755 the Mennonites of central Lancaster County had written to the Assembly that they had not realized all the implications of the promises they had made when being naturalized because none of them had been sufficiently acquainted with the English tongue then. The translation of the oath offered "by some of our own people" was later found "to be very wrong." As a result, they now needed to make clear the fact that while they could "with utmost fidelity acknowledge George upon the British Throne to be our lawful King and Sovereign," and would with "Cheerfulness" pay taxes laid down by "the Laws of Great Britain," they could never defend the King or laws "with Sword in hand." To their horror, they discovered that they had in ignorance of what they were signing promised to "maintain the Title and Reign of his Majesty . . . with Heart, Hands, and Life." But they now declared that they could not, in conscience, comply with such terms.

"It is our fixed principle," they wrote, "rather than take up Arms to defend our King, our Country, or our Selves, to suffer all that is dear to us to be rent from us, even Life itself, and this we think not out of Contempt to Authority, but that herein we act agreeable to what we think is the mind and Will of our Lord Jesus." This was said, they noted, not out of any dislike for the Assembly or the Governor, but only out of "a Sense of the command of God upon us forbidding us to take up Arms against any." It was a testimony they would maintain throughout the

stormy Revolutionary era, and one which the Amish have
kept unbroken for the 200 years of the new nation's
existence.

Returning now to the Skippack community from which
we have watched the sending of relief-wagons, we find its
domestic life unruffled. One of Andrew Ziegler's sons has
found a watch in the road to Skippack, and the minister
notifies editor Saur to mention the fact in his paper, the
person correctly describing it to be given the watch for
the price of the notice. A month later Andrew's father-in-
law, the wealthy preacher Dielman Kolb, dies and as sole
heir Andrew becomes a landholder of considerable importance. As a saddler, however, he owns fewer cattle
than the average farmer in the neighborhood. Another
local death is that of Bishop Henry Funk's wife, Anna,
and the widower soon thereafter writes his own will, in his
native German, laying down explicit instructions for the
disposition of his large holdings and the care of his lame
daughter Esther. "It falls heavily on me," he writes, "to
see how to order all things rightly."

The bishop is burdened with "a presentiment that the
time of my departure may be near at hand," and yet he is
apprehensive lest those he leaves behind fail to act "in ac-
cordance with brotherly love, Christian forbearance and
righteousness." The Funks are strong-willed people, and
there has been friction between him and his deacon
brother-in-law Christian Meyer. Yet it is to the deacon
that he must leave the final guarantee of care for Esther,
should, by some chance, the Funk family neglect her. As
to any debts that may be outstanding against his estate,
the executors are to try to collect them "in the same way
as I have always done—by using no force against any

man; and what is lost, or is regarded as lost, may be lost . . . which point I desire may not be forgotten." However, if any of the children should for any reason fail to comply with the terms of their father's will, "it will be well to make use of the instituted laws against them."

A year later, in June, 1760, Henry Funk's will was executed and each of his four sons now owned a farm or mill. An era was ended; the Franconia Mennonites had lost their most articulate leader. Strangely, the first bishop they had ordained in America, Jacob Gaedtschalck, a carpenter on whose farm was located the Towamencin meetinghouse, was still living, though now enfeebled and beginning his nineties. Successors to both Henry and Jacob were necessary. The miller-author, whose last manuscript lay in his house unpublished, was replaced by Andrew Ziegler's brother-in-law, the tall and physically powerful Isaac Kolb, minister at the Rockhill meetinghouse, which stood between his and his brother-in-law Michael Derstine's farms. Of Isaac it was storied that he had once helped at a house-raising frolic where the discussion had turned, at mealtime, on whether two or four horses would be required to move a certain large beam. The workers had been astounded, after the meal, to see Isaac nonchalantly shoulder the beam himself and walk off with it. Shortly after his ordination to the office of bishop, Isaac surprised a large meeting of ministers by declaring heatedly that he would not serve as bishop with Christian Meyer (a "confirmed" or senior deacon), since the deacon had made things difficult for the departed bishop Henry Funk. Christian was considerably put out by this but could effect no change in Isaac's determination. Personal differences in this society where everyone was somehow related by blood to everybody else could play a surprisingly prominent role in the life of the church.

The year of Isaac's ordination as bishop also brought into the consciousness of Pennsylvanians a new king, George the Third, proclaimed with great drinking of healths and other celebrations in the polite city of Philadelphia, thirty miles south of Indian Creek.

The next year, 1762, a bishop was ordained to take up the work of Jacob Gaedtschalck in the area toward Skippack. The choice fell on none other than Andrew Ziegler, Isaac Kolb's outspoken brother-in-law, son of a Lutheran immigrant who had joined the Mennonite fellowship in America and been ordained one of their first deacons. Both Isaac and Andrew had been ministers since their twenties, and were now in their fifties. With the death, a year later, of Bishop Gaedtschalck, who had been born in 1670 and had been ordained in the original settlement of Germantown in 1702, the last direct link with the earliest leadership of their American fellowship was severed. Jacob had been able to recall the first organization of the church, the letters to Holland for advice, the preliminary difficulty of reconciling Dutch with Palatine-Swiss manners. The new generation would now face internal tensions of another kind, as the American populace would polarize in an as yet unimaginable way, and pull into its oppositions even the "Dutch Mennonists" who did not believe in war.

A sign of these times was the building of stone meetinghouses and homes, whereas the first ones had been made of logs. A stage line now ran from Philadelphia to Bethlehem, not far from the farm of Henry Funk, Jr., on which the Perkasie (Blooming Glen) meetinghouse had

been built a decade earlier. Henry Funk, Jr.'s, brother
Abraham, who had inherited their father's mill along the
Indian Creek, now sold it to his preacher-brother Christian, and moved north to Springtown, where he was to
prosper conspicuously on a farm and mill. The sons of the
departed bishop also arranged to have their father's
considerable manuscript published in Philadelphia. It
contained twenty-five chapters explaining "several chief
points of the Law," the basic thesis being that Christ is
the fulfillment of the Old Testament Law, which will become evident in fullness at the Day of Judgment. The
centuries-old Mennonite teaching on Christian "defence-
lessness" was kept as vigorous as ever. "Jesus gives a
beautiful teaching," wrote the bishop, "where He calls
His followers sheep [and] lambs. . . . It is well known that
sheep and lambs have no nature to kill or persecute the
wolves or their enemies, and when the sheep and lambs
have no way of escape, they let themselves be caught and
killed by their enemies or wolves."

Several months after the publication of their deceased
bishop's book the Franconia Mennonites received news
of the most shocking riot their colony had yet seen. It was
the increasingly familiar story of frontier Scotch-Irish
"Presbyterians" rebelling against an eastern-dominated
Assembly and its lenient policy toward the Indians. On a
cold, snowy morning in December of 1763 a gang of men
from along the Susquehanna, popularly called the
"Paxton Boys," stormed into a village of peaceful Christian Delaware Indians living near the farms of Benjamin
Hershey and John Brubaker west of Lancaster Town.
Their goal was murder, and they left behind fourteen
scalped Indians in their burnt cabins. Little Christy's gun

was seen in their hands when they left, bloody tomahawks tied to their saddles. One Indian child had been hid by his mother under a barrel, with instructions to make no noise. The child obeyed, even though the poor thing's arm was broken by a suspicious shot fired at the barrel by one of the bloodthirsty raiders.

This butchery was the rough frontierman's response to Indian raids in their own community. They now wished to see the red man exterminated in their territory and its environs, and were infuriated whenever they saw white people treating the Indians as friends. Benjamin Hershey and John Brubaker overheard them discussing their next move—a raid on the Lancaster jail, where the twenty-eight Indians who had not been at home during the massacre had been placed for their own safety. Benjamin and John went to the Lancaster authorities in agitated secrecy to report the plot. But the magistrates, for a variety of trivial reasons, could not be found, and the Paxton Boys, breaking into the jail unopposed, murdered all twenty-eight Indians—old men, women, and children included. No matter that they had been taught basketmaking by local people and had given up all interest in war. The only good Indian was a dead Indian. With forty-two scalps in their possession, the Paxton Boys boasted that they would head next for Philadelphia, where more Indians were being protected, and teach the pious Quakers a lesson. During these fearful days Benjamin Hershey's son Christian hid two old Indians, "Michael and Mary," in the cellar of his farmhouse in nearby Manheim Township.

The poor Moravian-converted Indians at Philadelphia were speedily lodged in barracks, and cannon planted

around them. To the consternation of Quaker leaders,
about 200 of their members, mostly young men, took up
arms to challenge the approaching rioters. As reports of
their coming thickened, bells tolled and Benjamin
Franklin prepared to go to Germantown to meet them
with reason as well as force if necessary. Out in Norriton
the grandson of a former Mennonite minister at Germantown was working in his clockmaker's shop along the
Germantown Road. In 1756, during the period of Indian
raids, the young genius had been so engrossed in making
telescopes that, he confessed, he could hardly take the Indian troubles seriously. But this commotion was inescapa-
ble. "About fifty of the scoundrels marched by my work-
shop," wrote David Rittenhouse. "I have seen hundreds
of Indians traveling the country, and can with truth affirm that the behavior of these fellows was ten times more
brutal and savage than theirs."

After giving Germantown the severest scare it had ever
had, most of the Paxton Boys turned west again without
firing a shot, having been persuaded by Franklin that
they would get nowhere by offering further violence. But
there was grave foreboding in the minds of weighty
Friends of Philadelphia. What was coming over peaceful
Pennsylvania? "The Presbyterians are active, nu-
merous," complained one Quaker in a letter, "and are
trying to get a majority in the Assembly." Indeed they
were. They were tired of being outvoted by coalitions of
English Quakers and German Mennonites. One politician
from Philadelphia wrote to another in Lancaster advising
him to spread the word that they would "thrash" every
Quaker or Mennonite who came to the polls on election
day "to a jelly." The poll-watchers were to carry "shil-

lelaghs," and be obvious about it. That would settle the hash of the conscientious Mennonites. "I am well assured," added the Philadelphia strategist, "not a third of the Mennonists are naturalized," and thus, he reasoned, they should not be allowed to carry any weight in an election. Finally, the letter-writer begged that "no mention be made of the author" of these intriguing instructions.

Thus there was enough trouble in the world outside the Franconia Mennonite community without its nursing any friction in its own bosom. Yet Bishop Isaac Kolb, unhappy with his colleague Christian Meyer, sold his farm at Rockhill and bought another near the Quakers of Gwynedd Township, where a Mennonite meetinghouse was built on the flat lands called "Plains."

The war with the French and the Indians was now over, with Great Britain the decisive victor. All should have been well for the Colonies, as tranquillity returned to the frontier and the Indians sullenly retreated. Yet the resolution of one sort of trouble seemed to breed new kinds. The Scotch-Irish were angry that by the terms of the peace they were not allowed to settle west of the Appalachians. The British, for their part, were determined that the Colonies should stop fussing over intercolonial jealousies and help to pay the bill for their own military defense. An orderly way to collect revenue for defense was called for.

And so, on November 1, 1765, a stamp tax was levied, with the amazing result that the Colonies roared like an angry hydra-headed monster. Expressions like "the chains forged for us" and "insupportable slavery" were heard in fiery speeches. Perplexed, Parliament repealed the law four or five months later, but not before even peaceful Quakers questioned the wisdom of "taxation without representation." Israel Pemberton, reporting to a London friend a spirit of anarchy and confusion in Philadelphia, included the information that the Schwenk-felders had requested advice from London on how best to respond to the touchy issue.

Meanwhile, the mill wheel turns steadily beside the Indian Creek where Christian Funk is becoming the richest farmer in Franconia. The Stamp Act is no great concern of his, nor of Bishop Isaac Kolb, retired in Gwynedd, nor of Andrew Ziegler, saddler of Salford. The Scriptures are clear on such matters. "Render unto Caesar the things which are Caesar's." The King's laws are ordained of God. Taxes are to be paid.

Chapter 2

A Shadow of the Coming Storm

The peace of Pennsylvania, one of the few Colonies not directly under the king's government, was generally undisturbed in the decade leading up to the famous Boston Tea Party in 1773. The Indians had now been reduced to a factor of minor importance. The only ones left in Lancaster County, Michael and Mary, lived out their lives in a wigwam on Christian Hershey's farm, where the wrinkled old Delaware grandmother laughed in childlike joy to hear a visiting Moravian missionary speak to her in her native tongue. Governor John Penn issued the old couple a special certificate of protection soon after the Paxton massacre.

Tensions did not abate entirely, however. At the ruined Indian village five or six miles south of the Hershey farm, where the Conestogas had been assassinated by the Paxton Boys, another Mennonite, Jacob Whisler, had been appointed by the Proprietors of Pennsylvania as overseer. This was part of his larger commission "to superintend and take care of the unsold parts of Conestoga Manor," from the sale of which the Proprietors expected further income. To Jacob's consternation, a squatter named Robert Poke built a cabin at the site of one that had been burned, the home of an Indian called Jo Hayes. Jacob had, in line with his commission, allowed one Thomas Fisher to live on part of the land, to help in maintaining the ownership of the Proprietors of this section of the "Manor lands." Mennonite immigrants expected to pay for the acres they settled, and Scotch-Irish "squatting" seemed to them a form of lawbreaking.

While stopping one morning in January of 1766 at the mill of his neighbor Abraham Herr, Jacob noticed the irregular Robert Poke buying "a Kegg of Spirituous Liquor" from the miller. While some Mennonites (such as Deacon Christian Meyer of Franconia) were distillers and had no scruples as yet regarding the moderate use of liquor, they discountenanced the keeping of public houses because where liquor was convivially consumed, as a form of recreation, scandalous behavior was a constant threat. Jacob's unpleasant impressions of Poke were suddenly confirmed when he returned home in the afternoon and his wife informed him that the lawful inhabitant, Thomas Fisher, had been there with the urgent news that the dreaded Paxton men had come to Robert Poke's, and that Jacob was to go to Fisher's house immediately. Taking with him Martin Stauffer for support, Jacob hurried to Fisher's, where he found twenty-five or thirty rude men carrying powder horns and pouches, "and some of them guns."

A young man who called himself their captain stepped forward, when Jacob and Martin entered the house, and demanded in menacing tones what right Jacob had to place Thomas Fisher on the abandoned Indian land. Several of the men angrily requested that he show them the papers, and Jacob replied that he did not choose to show them to the whole company, who might "take or destroy them," but that if two or three of them would come with him to his home, he would produce the papers there. The young "captain," an elderly man, and another man whom Jacob recognized as a Mr. Bayley then went to his home, where he allowed them to read over his commission. As soon as they were finished they pronounced the papers "good for nothing." The governor and the proprietors, they insisted with their frontier outlook, had no right to the land, as it had belonged to the Indians, and since they were now dead, it belonged to those who had killed them.

Continuing their angry talk, the three men warned Jacob to give up his concerns with the land, and not to let the government officials know of their company's proceedings. When they handed back the papers the older man took Jacob aside and advised him "in a pretended friendly manner" to have nothing more to do with the land. If he did, he could "depend upon it, they would do him some great mischief." Jacob, realizing that he would have to give an account of these doings, asked the third man if his name were not Bayley, but received no reply. Just before leaving his house, the two leaders informed Jacob that all the Paxton men had "sworn to obey and stand by" whatever their captains directed.

All this and more Jacob Whisler was to recite, a week later, as he stood before William Allen, Chief Justice of the Province of Pennsylvania. Refusing to take an oath, the Mennonite witness nevertheless gave his sober affir-

mation that his testimony was the truth. Many of the justices of Pennsylvania were by now familiar with the
scruples on this point held by Quakers and the
nonresistant German sects. It was a common Pennsylvania phenomenon that would not have been tolerated in
some other areas of the Colonies. What would have been
bewildering to a European observer was actually working
in Penn's Holy Experiment. The confusing variety of
belief and practice of the Colony's Christians was produc-
ing less internal strife than had been common in the Old
World. "You can hardly imagine," wrote Christopher
Schultz, wealthy Schwenkfelder preacher-farmer near
Hereford in Berks County, "how many denominations
you will find here when you are attending a big gathering. . . . We are all going to and fro like fish in water but
always at peace with each other. . . . Everybody speaks his
mind freely. A Mennonite preacher [John Bechtel] is my
nearest neighbor and I could not wish for a better one; on
the other side I have a big Catholic church. The present
Jesuit father . . . confides in me more than in those who
come to him for confession. . . ." The only negative aspect of all this, Schultz observed, was the difficulty of
each group's instructing its children in its own beliefs.

There was, indeed, a certain amount of crossing over
from ancestral denominations to other varieties, as
children grew up and found wives and husbands on
neighboring farms of interweaving communities. The
Dunkards, especially, were evangelistic in spirit, and
gained more than they lost in interchange. The earliest
experience of the Mennonites in Germantown had been
of conversion to Quakerism. In some cases such conver-
sions had even occurred before emigration from Europe.

This had led to the anomaly of a group of Quakers writing a protest, in 1688, against the practice of their members holding slaves, the signatures to which turned out to be mostly traditional Mennonite names.

One of the most interesting cases involving the descendant of a Mennonite family who grew away from Mennonite views and fellowship was that of the young astronomer David Rittenhouse, by whose roadside shop in rural Norriton the rowdy Paxton Boys had tramped on their way to Germantown. David's father, Mathias, had been born and raised at the site of the old Rittenhouse paper mill in the Cresheim Creek Valley of Germantown. Mathias's father, Claus, had been one of the ministers of the Mennonite meeting there, following his father William, the first Mennonite to be ordained in America. But Mathias had married one of the local Quaker girls, Wilhemina Dewees, and had moved with his young family out into Norriton Township where he was farming near his brother, Henry, a Mennonite who gave land for the building of a meetinghouse at "Madetchy" (Methacton). Mathias hardly knew what to make of his son, David, who had constructed a miniature windmill by the age of eight, and decorated the handles of his plow as he walked along behind the horses with chalked mathematical formulae. At eighteen he made a clock, and the father, disappointed in not having a farmer son, allowed him to buy clockmaker's tools in Philadelphia and set up a shop out along the road.

A young Episcopalian schoolteacher who courted and won David's sister introduced the clockmaker to some books whereby he taught himself sufficient Latin to read Isaac Newton's famous *Principia,* and rapidly soared far beyond the imaginings of his country Mennonite cousins. By 1767 he was awarded an honorary Master of Arts degree by the College of Philadelphia for his amazing achievements in mechanics, mathematics, and astronomy. He had built into one of his clocks a small planetarium, and was now intent on devising a mechanical planetarium that would outclass anything like it in the world for accuracy and completeness. And still the neighbors gazed and still their wonder grew as the gears and levers were cut to the designs of David's own conception and calculation. Sun, moon, earth, and planets revolved against spangled blue heavens, a shining frame. The College of New Jersey enthusiastically placed its order for the unprecedented (in America) contraption.

As June 3, 1769, approached, the young astronomer grew feverish with intellectual excitement. The "transit of Venus"—the passage of the planet between the earth and the sun—was to take place during that Saturday afternoon, not to happen again for over a century. With delicate instruments some of which he had designed and calibrated by himself, David intended, if the afternoon were providentially free of clouds, to measure the elapsed time of the transit. From this and from other observations made by fellow scientists at two other points he would calculate the distance of the earth from the sun. On the farm his father had conveyed to him in Norriton he built a rude log observatory, and set up a telescope donated by William Penn's son John. Others with scientific interests gathered around him. As the historic afternoon arrived, a deep silence fell upon the observing crowd. The astronomer, whose health was shaky as a result of his youthful taxing of his body, worked intensely, communing with the heavenly machine he had for years been imitating. At five seconds after two o'clock the transit began. After it was completed and David had successfully registered time and distances, he was overcome with the tension, and passed out. His calculation of the sun's distance from the earth turned out to be the most accurate hitherto made by man, and reverberated among the scientific societies of Europe. In Philadelphia he was hailed as one of America's wonders.

As to religion, David spoke the language of Franklin rather than that of his Mennonite forebears. The Supreme Designer of the Universe rather than the crucified Christ was the object of his rational, nondenominational worship. As an increasingly popular Philadelphia figure, however, he would exercise an influence on new laws which would affect his Mennonite cousins, such as Wilhemina, wife of preacher Dielman Kolb the younger at Skippack.

Dielman's uncle Isaac, as we have seen, had proven unwilling or unable to work along with deacon Christian Meyer of Franconia, and there was also a question of his poor health. His first wife having died, he was nursed in his sickness by his daughter Elizabeth, wife of farmer Jacob Alderfer of Lower Salford. Living in Gwynedd among the Quakers, the elderly bishop had to travel from the outer edge of the Mennonite community to visit the central districts of Salford and Franconia. A new bishop was now called for by the ministers of Bechtel's (Rockhill), Indianfield (Franconia), and Clemens' (Salford). A vote was taken on which ministers should be candidates for casting lots to select a "confirmed" minister or bishop. The two names which emerged were

miller Christian Funk, and the purchaser of Strong Isaac
Kolb's Rockhill farm, Samuel Bechtel.

At this point deacon Christian Meyer objected to the
procedure, saying that in his opinion Isaac Kolb should
carry out his duties as bishop, which would make another
ordination unnecessary. This put Christian's nephew
Christian Funk and Samuel Bechtel in a difficult position: should they submit to the traditional casting of lots
by which one of them would be appointed bishop, when
one of their chief co-laborers was opposed to the move?
They consulted privately, and then agreed that it would
be best to accept the call for a casting of lots. Christian
Moyer continued to object, in spite of the other ministers'
fruitless urgings, but he was suddenly called out of the
room by his wife, who apparently changed his mind on
the spot. Upon his return he gave his consent for the ordination. When the lot fell on Christian Funk, the miller
was installed at once as the new bishop. Isaac Kolb, once
again reconciled to the idea of working with the Franconia congregation, "gave his assistance until death."

The three leading men in the councils of the oldest
large settlement of Mennonites in Pennsylvania were now
the retired Isaac Kolb; his brother-in-law, saddler
Andrew Ziegler; and miller Christian Funk. The latter, at
thirty-eight, was more than a decade younger than the
other two men, now in their fifties. But all three were sons
of minister, deacon, or bishop, and each had married the
daughter of a local ordained man. Christian's wife, Barbara, was the daughter of Yellis Cassel of the Skippack
congregation, who with his brother Hupert had brought
along from Europe the papers of their grandfather Yellis,
likewise a minister in the Palatinate. One of them

contained a lengthy poem by their ancestral leader, complaining to God of murders and pillage taking place in his rural Palatinate community during the 1670's.

The Franconia bishops doubtless reflected on the ironies of their having left Europe to escape such turmoils, when in March of 1770 news of a "massacre" in Boston whipped through the Colonies. This had come as a result of tensions building over the English government's continuing efforts to find a way by which the Colonies could be taxed to pay for their own defense. The hated Stamp Act having been repealed, Parliament had passed a series of other measures designed to produce revenue, referred to as the Townshend Acts, taxing such imports as glass and tea. But now the protests of American merchants rose more loudly than ever. In response, a law was made requiring American citizens to quarter the king's soldiers in their houses on demand. This was greeted with the greatest disgust of all, and before long a rabble of boys, fomented by angry adult radicals, had tormented some English troops standing in front of the Boston Court House into firing at the crowd. Five persons were killed, and shock waves rolled out through the Colonies. Lord North, the British Prime Minister, then decided to repeal the Townshend Duties, except for the one on tea, and a short period of better relations followed.

In these years, to use the words of minister and miller Christian Funk, Pennsylvania was "at rest." He himself had prospered to the point that he had more cattle than anyone else in Franconia Township. He was also listed in the assessor's records as having several indentured servants, as was the case with his Mennonite neighbor Georg Delp. Several Reformed families in the community

had their "Cuff" or "Betz," black slaves. The white indentured servants such as eighteen-year-old John Swartley, whose services were bought by Henry Rosenberger,
two farms up the Indian Creek from Funk's Mill, were in
a far freer state, even though they had to "serve out their
time" to pay their ocean passage. John, who arrived in
1772, was soon accepted as a prospective son-in-law, and
one of Andrew Ziegler's neighbors, the Lutheran servant
Frederick Alderfer, had actually married his employer's
widow, and was already a wealthy Mennonite farmer.

Frederick was now called upon, with Bishop Andrew
Ziegler, to execute the will of the saintly old schoolmaster
Christopher Dock, who had at last died "in his great
age," having lived to see what he would have preferred
not to. In the month of the "Boston Massacre" the Germantown newspaper editor, Christopher Saur, Jr., had rejoiced to discover in his shop a yellowed manuscript he
had feared lost forever. It was the twenty-year-old
description by Dock of his methods of school administration, written after considerable pleading by Saur and his
father. Dock, they believed, was a person of rare spirit,
and they wished to see his kindly manners and philosophy
imitated. Already imagining in 1750 that he was approaching the end of his life, he had hesitantly composed
his essay on school management then, asking that it be
published, if it must, only after his death. When Saur
later reported the manuscript lost in his printshop, Dock
told him not to worry. But suddenly, after Saur had ad-
vertised for them in vain, the papers turned up under his
nose, and he at once published them in his *Spiritual
Magazine*. Within the following year Christopher Dock
died, kneeling in prayer in his Skippack classroom, ac-

cording to local legend. Another era had closed.

A year and a half later (March 1773) Bishop Andrew Ziegler, who picked up his European mail in the stores of Philadelphia merchants, sat down with his fellow bishops Christian Funk and Isaac Kolb to answer a friendly inquiry from Mennonites in the Old Country, at Crefeld and Utrecht. These correspondents were curious about the condition, size, and practices of the Mennonite communities in the New World, the first permanent settlers of which had left Crefeld ninety years earlier. They wished to include this information in their publications describing European Mennonite communities. The bishops of Skippack, Indianfield, and Plains replied somewhat shyly, protesting that they represented an "unlearned people," who were generally "very deficient in writing." It was all they could do to keep proper records, in the midst of changing an Indian forest into an agricultural landscape. As to a history of the earliest stages of their blended Dutch and Swiss Mennonite community, all they had was a short written account left behind by Dutch-speaking Bishop Jacob Godshalk, who had died ten years earlier at Towamencin. They reviewed its contents for their Dutch inquirers, adding only two sentences to summarize their history from 1708 to 1773. They calculated the number of Mennonite bishops currently in America to be "at least eighteen," and the number of "communities" at fifty.

The blessings of prosperity and great freedom characterize their life in Pennsylvania, they report. "We even have some among us who are rich." They order their church life by the Bible without any further code of human regulations, they explain, though the previous

generation of bishops and ministers in America had endorsed the confession of faith drawn up by Mennonites at
Dordrecht in Holland in 1632. In civil and religious affairs they enjoy a very un-European "unlimited freedom," a legacy of William Penn's noble charter. Their
"praiseworthy magistrates" allow them to affirm the
truth of their testimony without taking an oath. They refrain from accepting offices in the government because
force is used in carrying out the law. If someone marries
out of the community, he or she is notified that the
covenant relationship has been broken, and can only be
renewed through proper expiation.

Then the three unschooled bishops turn the tables and
ask their more sophisticated Dutch friends what the letters "A.L.M. & Ph.D." mean on the picture of a Dutch
Mennonite minister of Amsterdam. They are curious also
as to whether the long-standing division among Dutch
Mennonites of various backgrounds is still in evidence,
and, if so, "whether they seek to bear themselves toward
each other in love."

This final inquiry would prove to be ironic, in retros-
pect, as a sad division would take place between two of
the very bishops who wrote this letter, and settle into a
bitterness which would curse their children's peace.
Christian Funk and Andrew Ziegler were schooled from
childhood in the teaching that love, as they wrote to their
European colleagues, "is the greatest command," and
that therefore Christians must refrain from hatred of any
kind, above all, war. Yet, after first reacting with deep
dismay at the coming of a war against their own sovereign
king, they would find themselves impossibly at odds
among each other as to how, as a church, they should re-

concile the conflicting demands of two Caesars who were both claiming to be rendered unto at once.

A shadow of the coming storm fell across their peace when the news arrived, nine months after their cheerful letter was written, that a British ship with a cargo of tea had been sent back down the Delaware unloaded from the port of Philadelphia. Captain Ayres, of the *Polly*, had been advised that he would find himself "in hot water" if he tried to leave his tea on the docks. "What think you, Captain," queried a sarcastic handbill, "of a Halter around your Neck—ten Gallons of liquid Tar decanted on your Pate—with the feathers of a dozen wild Geese laid over that to enliven your Appearance?" Philadelphia hotheads, who had been in touch with Sam Adams of Boston and the secret organization called the Sons of Liberty, considered the arrival of the tea a ploy by which the despicable British tax could be reimposed, and they stated flatly that "no Power on the face of the Earth" had "a right to tax them" without their consent. If the Mennonite bishops considered such a defiance of the king's laws perplexing, the issue was even more sharply drawn less than a month later, when angry Boston men disguised as Indians deliberately hurled 342 chests of tea into their own harbor.

Parliament was of course outraged, and after an inconclusive debate agreed that New England must now be taught a decisive lesson. The Boston port was shut down as of June 1774, the first of a series of acts which New England patriots soon called "Intolerable." Their response to such punishment was to call for the sympathy of their fellow American Colonials, and in mid-May Paul Revere arrived on horseback in Philadelphia, bearing a

written appeal for Pennsylvanians to aid the suffering
Massachusetts Colony. Immediately a call was issued by
Philadelphia patriots for the creation of "committees of
correspondence," to be organized on the model of the
original one set up several months earlier by Sam Adams
in Massachusetts, to keep information flowing swiftly
among patriot groups.

Within a month such a committee was formed in the
courthouse in Lancaster, and within days its members attended a meeting of some 8,000 people in Philadelphia.
Petitions to Governor John Penn for a special session of
the Pennsylvania Assembly had been ignored. Thus
leaders whom elected officials sniffed at as being "self-
appointed" decided to set a day for a convention of
representatives from committees of correspondence all
over the colony. Seventy-five delegates from eleven
counties did arrive in Philadelphia on July 15, and stayed
for a week of sessions, issuing sixteen resolutions in support of the rebellious Bostonians and stating that the
powers claimed by the British Parliament were "fundamentally wrong." It was agreed that there was "an
absolute necessity for an immediate congress" of representatives from all the Colonies to meet the growing
crisis. No one said anything about so radical a thing as independence from the mother country, except to condemn
the very thought. It was the rights of free citizens, not independence, that were sought.

A *congress*, convening from all the Colonies to take action against the king! A daring idea and clearly illegal.

From every Colony but Georgia, one did gather in
early September, in the City of Brotherly Love, thirty
miles south of Indian Creek. Among its delegates was

John Adams of Massachusetts, with his more inflammable cousin Sam. Together they had been escorted jubilantly out of the city of Boston by citizens who wished them success in winning the rest of the Colonies to the support of besieged Massachusetts. Radicals in the new Congress swung the vote against meeting in the State House of Pennsylvania, even though the Assembly had offered it for their use. The radicals wished to demonstrate their independence of the conservative Quaker-dominated regular legislature. Meeting from the first week in September to the last week in October, they called for a voluntary "Association" of patriots in each colony, to stop all trade with the British and the consumption of British goods. Let the arrogant British learn a lesson! If Parliament would cut off Americans from ocean traffic, why, let the English have their merchandise. Americans would grow and manufacture their own supplies. Patriotic women could do without tea, and could knit stockings for their servants. The American men would make their own guns and buy type for their printing presses from an ingenious inventor in Germantown.

John Adams, the future President of an as yet unthought of nation, did not like everything he heard or saw at the Congress. An intellectual lawyer from Bucks County, Joseph Galloway, proposed the moderate plan of a federal union between Britain and the American Colonies. This seemed to Adams like a surrender of the trump card to unscrupulous opponents. Nor was he at all pleased by his encounter one evening with a group of Philadelphia Quakers. He went with his colleagues to Carpenter's Hall at six o'clock, upon the invitation of some "gentlemen" who had been talking to Baptists from

his home state and said they "wished to communi-
cate . . . a little business" to the Congregational delegates. Adams was surprised to find the hall nearly full of
men, with many Quakers seated at a long table, wearing
their broad-brimmed beaver hats. After Adams' group
had sat down among them, the Quakers said that they
had received complaints from their meetings in Massachusetts, and from Baptists there as well, regarding the
legally enforced payment of taxes to support the Massachusetts Congregationalist Church. There had been
court trials (John Adams was involved in them himself) at
which the law had been made to stick.

With rising irritation Adams heard the devout and
wealthy Israel Pemberton, sometimes called "King of the
Quakers," say that the Friends considered state-church
laws to be a breach of their treasured liberty of conscience, and that as far as Pennsylvanians were concerned
this would be of chief importance in subscribing to any
kind of union of Colonies. Quakers could not approve of
such religious laws, requiring people to support churches
they did not attend, as in New England. Adams immediately typed Friend Pemberton as a tricky politician,
who was using this issue to break up the Congress. He
considered the Quaker majority in the Pennsylvania
Assembly to be the result of unfair representation, and
had no intention of being lectured to on freedom of
conscience by a group of people he felt had unjustly taken
"the whole power of the State" into their hands.
Heatedly he rose and told Pemberton that the people of
Massachusetts were as religious and conscientious as the
people of Pennsylvania, and that if the Quakers insisted
on imposing Pennsylvania ideas on the people of Massa-

chusetts, who firmly intended to keep their "meeting house and Sunday laws," they had better not prate of freedom of conscience.

"Oh! sir," returned the annoyed Friend Pemberton, "pray don't urge liberty of conscience in favor of such laws." Equally dismayed must have been the listening Baptists from Rhode Island, as they heard Adams defending what to them amounted to religious oppression. However, unlike the Quakers, they were quite ready to join ranks with those who opposed what was coming to be called the tyranny of the English king.

The Congress did not let the keeping of its resolutions to the general whims of the public. To make sure that directions regarding the "Association" were kept, Congress called for every town or city to elect a "Committee of Observation," to keep watch on who was cooperating with the new measures, and who was not. Trade with the British, or consumption of British goods were to be condemned as traitorous, and reported to the local committees. Things had come to the point where American citizens were being asked, in effect, to spy on each other. Especially in the town of Lancaster, where a dozen of the leading men formed the new committee, would such work become complicated, as a large constituency of Mennonites, Quakers, Moravians, and other "conscientious scruplers" came under criticism as "Non-associators."

But perhaps most ominous of all was the gathering on the fringes of British-occupied Boston of 20,000 freemen of Massachusetts, in straggling array, to give the British General Gage a scare. They drew up a set of fiery anti-British "Resolves," and sent them, downright insulting as they were, to the Congress meeting in Philadelphia. To the shocked surprise of many observers, Congress ratified them, insults and all. It was a revolutionary gesture without precedent in America, and Bishop Christian Funk was as gravely suspicious of it as anybody.

Chapter 3

Associate or Contribute!

As soon as the Continental Congress published its proceedings, reported one Philadelphia Quaker to an English Friend, "the spirit of party raged with redoubled violence and spread like contagion. . . ." In every large town committees of observation began to operate. Farmers were instructed not to butcher their sheep before the wool was fully grown, and small factories sprang up for making gunpowder, nails, paper, and other items formerly imported. Handbills containing unfamiliar instructions from "committees" not elected by due course of law began to appear throughout the countryside, where Mennonite farm families reacted in dumb amazement.

The Quakers had a traditional way of responding to emergencies, which they called their "Meeting for Sufferings." Under these auspices they issued several pamphlets designed to dampen the alarming "party Spirit" and warn against a proposed convention at Philadelphia which, it was said, was intended to call Pennsylvanians to "learn the art of war" and "furnish

themselves with warlike weapons." The pamphlets were
printed in both English and German. Even before they
appeared, three Mennonite leaders called on their
Quaker friends at Gwynedd, several miles from the farm
of Bishop Isaac Kolb, to discuss the worsening situation
as they had once conferred over the Indian troubles. Pennsylvania had never had a compulsory military organization. Men who had formed associations for the pursuit of
martial training in the French and Indian War had done
so voluntarily, and thus the nonresistant or defenseless
Christians (the term used by the Mennonites) had not
felt strong pressures on their young men in former wars.

But the present situation seemed more ominous. On
February 9, 1775, King George III had actually declared
Massachusetts to be in a state of rebellion. British General
Gage, occupying the port of Boston with thousands of
soldiers, was hemmed in by an informal but effective
collection of militiamen from surrounding counties. It
was, for all practical purposes, a budding civil war, with
the populace divided in its loyalties. Many Americans
who had been deeply angered by the "Intolerable Acts"
were nevertheless totally out of sympathy with the tactic
of armed rebellion.

On April 19 it came to blood, when a force of 700 or
more British soldiers marched out from Boston to capture
guns and ammunition collected by the illegally organized
militia. On their way they met some armed farmers at
Lexington, and there was a sudden exchange of gunfire.
Another fight burst out in nearby Concord, and all during
the return march toward Boston muskets flashed from behind buildings and trees, leaving the Redcoats with 273
casualties.

This was war. No one knew, nor did it matter, who had fired the very first shot. General Gage now acknowledged open rebellion, and set about trying to catch the "incendiaries," Sam Adams and John Hancock. The patriots flung back accusations of "butchery" and "barbarous murders on . . . our innocent brethren," committed "without any provocation." Express riders carried the news in every direction throughout the Colonies, where new military associations sprang into existence. Within weeks the people of Philadelphia were "warmed. . . almost to a military frenzy." Nine thousand Associators gathered in one meeting, and the whole town was "filled with companies exercising," their artillery and powder guarded every night. Peaceful Quakers were now doubly scorned for their stand, and those who dared to object openly to the new passion for liberty were called "Tories"—a venom-loaded epithet. One eminent Philadelphia doctor who spoke critically of the excesses of the opposite or "Whig" party was tarred and feathered, driven about in a cart, and, though he sputtered with vehement indignation, drummed out of the city.

As the new polarization spread to Pennsylvania's back country, defenseless Christians regarded it at first as just another worldly attitude from which they must stay aloof. But their military-minded neighbors soon demanded confrontation or silence. One young Mennonite learned to keep his mouth shut several weeks after the news of bloodshed at Lexington and Concord had reached his community in York County. He had been helping at a house-raising, when a local tavern-keeper named Michael Smyser announced that all the able-bodied men at the frolic were required to join some militia company, or else "be ranked among the Tories." The Mennonite youth then spoke up and advised against such warlike "mustering," saying that it would lead to actions that would later be regretted.

Mr. Smyser, who was also a militia captain, angrily stormed into the town of York, registered a complaint with the new County Committee of Observation, and secured from them a request for the immediate appearance before them of the Mennonite war critic. When the sobered young fellow had been hastily summoned from the frolic, the chairman, Colonel Thomas Hartley, first had Captain Smyser repeat the charges. Then he asked the accused what he had to say for himself. The only reply was that he had not considered his comments to have been injurious to anyone, in intent or effect. After the committee consulted briefly, Colonel Hartley announced that the young Mennonite was to be considered "an enemy to his country," and that, as a Tory, he was to be tarred and feathered.

This was just the kind of amusement a collection of local men and boys would welcome. Someone had already set a tar box, of the type carried on wagons, in front of the courthouse. One boy had mischievously brought along a feather-stuffed pillow. But when the young Mennonite, under orders from the committee, came and stood beside the tarbox, no one, including the boys, would approach him to apply the tar. Only one of the committee, an exceptionally rough man, had stayed to observe the results of their orders. A bystander concluded that the other committee-members were ashamed of the proceedings, and had thus disappeared.

Finally the man stated that the defenseless young critic

must tar himself, if no one else would do so. To this
ridiculous order the victim actually responded, taking off
his jacket and shirt. He had obediently stuck his fingers
into the tar and was dabbing it on his shoulder when
several of the boys, their sympathies somewhat mixed,
called out that he should let the man who had given the
order do the tarring himself. This brought the proceedings to a brief standstill. The sticky-fingered young Mennonite looked dubiously over the crowd for a moment,
and one of them suggested that he pick up his jacket and
shirt and go home. He immediately took this advice, and
began walking down the middle of the street. At this
someone ripped open the pillow and half-heartedly
hurled the feathers after him, but none seemed to stick. A
few small fellows traipsed behind him for a while, but by
the time he had walked a hundred yards he was alone,
and no mob had formed. There were simply too many
people who considered such things beneath them, or who
thought the whole war was foolishness, for the incident to
blossom into a full-scale punishment of a dissenter. The
radicals had not yet sufficiently polarized the populace.

Nearer to Philadelphia the issue was more inflamed.
Only two days earlier the committee of the town of
Lancaster had announced their own new association in
response to Great Britain's resorting to arms. Their language too had become fiery. Referring to the hated acts of
recent years as "most unjust, tyrannical, and cruel," the
committee had declared that they would not "become an
easy prey to them, or tamely submit and bend our necks
to the yoke prepared for us." Acting "under the deepest
sense of our duty to God, our country, ourselves, and
posterity," the members of the new association pledged

"to acquaint ourselves with military discipline and the art of war. . . ."

Drilling to the sound of fife and drum was the most obvious aspect of military discipline. As to the art of war, few Lancaster County men would need training in marksmanship. Further, they had the use of the deadliest small firearm in the world, the Pennsylvania rifle, often called the Kentucky rifle. Historians would one day trace its earliest design to the smithy of a Mennonite living a few miles from Lancaster—Martin Meylin. Though he had drawn on his Swiss heritage to make a gun serviceable to his fellow human beings, rather than for use against them, defenseless Martin would see the successors of his invention become, in the hands of his militant American brothers, "the most fatal widow-and-orphan makers in the world."

Still residing a mile west of Lancaster town was the elderly bishop Benjamin Hershey. The respected leader and spokesman of his people, Hershey had been born and raised in Europe, but had lived on Lancaster County soil for nearly sixty years. He had signed the petition for military exemption of his Mennonite community in 1755, when war with the French was approaching. Just below his signature had appeared the name of deacon Jacob Boehm, whose son Martin was now, two decades later, worrying Benjamin by his "Methodistic" preaching. Boehm had been ordained a bishop, but had been in contact with people from Virginia and other communities whose emphasis on "heart" religion somehow allowed Christ's teaching against violence to be seen as not applying to war. Bishop Boehm was ready to cooperate in his evangelism with Methodists who regarded war and the swearing of oaths as regrettable necessities, rather than completely forbidden, as his and Bishop Hershey's church had held for 2½ centuries.

While Benjamin pondered the new militancy of Lancaster a second session of the Continental Congress converged in Philadelphia. It was called in haste in response to the outbreaks at Lexington and Concord. When John Adams and his cousin Sam returned for this fateful meeting, they were astonished at the prevalent martial spirit, with 2,000 Philadelphians, including even some Quakers, marching about in daily drills. This time the Congress did more than pass resolutions. It decided, on the motion of John Adams, to "adopt" the militia gathered around Boston, and, against his wishes, appointed a gentleman farmer from Virginia named George Washington to be the commander-in-chief. To pay for the support of the army, Congress decided to issue $2,000,000 in paper money, the plates for which were promptly engraved by Paul Revere. The spreading of these new bills would carry the issue of rebellion directly into the markets and houses of Mennonite farmers.

During these deliberations, the peace of Lancaster was endangered by angry confrontations. Men who favored military associations and were mustering for drilling became indignant when they found that a great many of their neighbors refused, on grounds of conscience, to take up arms. Further, it was reported that "a few persons" in the communities through which the militia marched had been making insulting remarks about the recruits, calling them lazy, and saying that they would "follow the drum from an idle disposition." This trading of accusations alarmed the Committee of Observation. They met to hear the complaint of a company of militia formed in the heavily Mennonite townships of Manheim and Rapho, but before they broke up "two of the chief persons of the Menonists" came too, stating that some of their men had been threatened so severely that they were afraid to stay at their daily work. Members of the committee commented "that probably such conduct had partly arose from abusive or opprobrious language" directed by the defenseless Christians against the companies of armed militiamen. The Mennonites disclaimed such rude language, and even said that they would not object to members of their own group taking up arms, if their consciences were free to do so (which would automatically remove them from membership in the church).

The committee, feeling gratified that they had had a rational interchange with two aggrieved parties, decided to publish a handbill calling for moderation and respect on both sides of the association issue. Accordingly, they sumbitted a 200-word statement to a local printer, telling him to make copies in both English and German.

By the time these bills were ready for posting, three days later, the five military companies in the town of Lancaster were mustering for a drill. When the printer delivered the bills to a member of the committee, he reported that one of the association officers had tried to take them from his house by force. Shortly afterward, another officer rushed up to the committee-member's house and said that his men were "greatly dissatisfied" with the committee for having had such a middle-of-the-road bill printed. They would, in fact, refuse to muster for a drill "if any people whatever were excused from bearing arms and associating." The officer apologized for the men's behavior, and asked if there was not something that could be done to allay the public discontent. At this the committeeman suggested that if "ten or a dozen" of the militiamen wished to talk over calmly with the Committee the matter of the bill he would assure them a sympathetic hearing. The officer then left politely.

Less than five minutes later the sound of marching was heard in the town square, as one of the militia companies, barely in control of their captain, advanced on the courthouse. When they arrived, their officer called a halt, but the soldiers yelled, "March on! march on!" and the officer left them in confusion. Guns in hand, the troops marched to the house of another member of the committee and demanded all the handbills. The first member, who had them at his house, then walked up and told the rioters that if one of their officers asked for a copy, "it would be delivered to him with pleasure," but that none would be given to an unruly body of armed men. An officer then followed the committeeman to his house, received a bill, and brought it out to his men.

Immediately, rough hands seized the paper, affixed it to the nearby whipping post, and several of the soldiers raised their guns and shot it to tatters. This noise put the town into "a great ferment," as the opponents of the bill harangued curious bystanders. Actually, none of the bills had yet been posted anywhere or handed out. When the turmoil had subsided somewhat, the scheduled drills began, but the ranks were only thinly filled. Some of the militia loitered around the square all evening, throwing out threats against the Committee. At ten o'clock they gathered in front of a committeeman's house, and the next morning his door was found tarred and feathered.

Deeply disturbed by this unrest, the committee met
and decided to resign. In the afternoon a new committee
was elected. Two days later, on Sunday morning, a
militant sermon was preached to a company of riflemen
under the command of Captain James Ross, meeting in
full uniform in the Presbyterian Church on East Orange
Street. The clergyman, John Carmichael of the Forks of
the Brandywine, addressed himself vigorously to the
questions agitating the town regarding a Christian's role
in war. He assured the riflemen that Jesus did not forbid
self-defense, and that, in fact, John the Baptist had not included the laying down of arms in his instructions of
soldiers to repentance. For two hours Carmichael at-
tacked the British and defended the holiness of the
American cause. Since the Boston Massacre, he declared,
"the very expression 'Redcoat' stinks in our nostrils." The
moral question has become simply whether or not Americans would "submit tamely to the galling yoke of per-
petual slavery." The Christian soldier, of course, must determine that the war in which he fights is "a just war,
conducted in a lawful, righteous manner."

As for those who mistakenly believe that as Christians
they cannot go to war on any occasion whatsoever, they
should be pitied for their ignorance, not persecuted, he
advised. Common sense would make it clear to them, if
they opened their minds, that when Jesus told us to turn
the other cheek He did not expect us to go any "farther
than is consistent with our own safety." When He taught
that we should love our enemies, He could not possibly
have meant that we should let them kill us, for that would
"thwart the original first great law of self-preservation."
Further, Mennonites who refused to go to war and yet

paid taxes, argued the Presbyterian, were playing a foolish trick on their consciences." Paying taxes simply enabled the government to do what they themselves refused to do.

Not for a moment could the preacher take the Mennonite views seriously. "The light of nature," the Bible, "the reason of things," and "the example of Christ" all proved the fallacy of nonresistance. With the ringing tones of a convinced American patriot he invoked God's blessing on the American uprising against a corrupt Parliament. "All the angels of heaven are on our side," he orated, "for we have truth and justice on our side."

Doubtless the militiamen were heartened to hear that their religion was in such harmonious accord with their politics.

Their boisterous, independent spirit was not to be contained by anybody's religious teachings. Captain Ross's company would hardly arrive at the front near Boston before General Washington himself would be "chagrined" by their riotous, even mutinous camp behavior. Had they listened to a preacher of the Moravians, who had just submitted a declaration of their principles to the Continental Congress, they would have heard sentiments precisely opposite those of the Reverend Mr. Carmichael. Even the well-known, if old-fashioned Lutheran minister, Henry Melchior Muhlenberg, took a far more questioning view of the military excitement. He observed in his own church "companies of the recently organized civil militia." As he traveled between Philadelphia and Reading he saw small boys "marching in companies with little wooden drums and wooden guns." What did it all mean? he wondered, and asked people their opinions.

The answer he received was that God had given the
people liberty which men were now taking away, and that
every right-minded provider for his family should protect
his house against the thieves of liberty, who might even
kill and destroy. Pastor Muhlenberg soon found that it
was downright dangerous to preach, as he believed, that
the present ills came from an abuse of freedom, a false se-
curity, and related sins. To say this would, he realized, be
inviting foolish people to call him a traitor. It would be
better simply to preach on topics that had no immediate
political application.

As the resentment of Associators toward nonsubscribers
grew, a shoemaker by the name of Criner was heard telling people near Reading that the Lancaster Committee
had received a bribe of 15,000 pounds to excuse the
Quakers and Mennonites from arming. When asked what
grounds he had for this statement, he replied that the fact
that whole denominations were excused en masse was
sufficient evidence. He even suggested the names of
three of the committee who were particularly suspected
of having taken the bribe.

Before it had even heard this report, the new committee called for a meeting of township committees in an attempt to restore the "harmony, peace, unanimity, and
good order" in which the various sects had always lived in
Lancaster County. The solution they proposed was for all
whose consciences would not allow them to equip
themselves with guns to contribute to the committee the
sum of three pounds ten shillings. And since those who
were willing to associate incurred additional expense because of the time spent away from their work while drilling, it was recommended that those with conscientious

scruples should pay to the treasurer of the committee an additional amount equal to the yearly tax assessment on their property. If everyone would do this voluntarily, there should be no more serious tensions.

But as long as this was a recommendation instead of a legally required tax, the Mennonites, Brethren, Amish, Moravians, Schwenkfelders, and Quakers had a problem. Contributing their three pounds ten shillings and their tax-equivalent would, for all practical purposes, be aiding a war effort they did not believe in. Helping refugees was something they had always done gladly, but could they now fill the war chest with voluntary contributions that were not even legally enforced?

Chapter 4

A Short and Sincere Declaration

Two days after George Washington had been commissioned by the Congress to take charge of the loosely organized American soldiers surrounding Boston, a vicious fight broke out on Breed's Hill, just across the bay. The British general, his campaign to put down rebellion already stymied, knew that he dared not lose these strategic heights, and so he paid the price of over a thousand casualties to maintain possession. The Americans, who were driven back off the hill they had tried to take, nevertheless now realized that they could throw a good scare into the British forces, who had previously told each other that the Yankees were cowards. Washington left Philadelphia within days after the battle, intent on whipping the ragtag militiamen into a disciplined fighting machine and pushing General Gage back onto his boats.

In Pennsylvania the news of "Bunker Hill" put a bellows to the flames of the war spirit. "It is almost impossible to describe the fervor for preservation of liberty which is now burning in North America," wrote

Schwenkfelder farmer Christopher Schultz. "Everyone
has taken up arms and in the villages even the smallest
lads organize companies and conduct military drills."
The more the militia drilled, the heavier grew the
pressure on non-drillers to contribute their three pounds
ten shillings. This "contribution" was regarded by many,
including the Moravians, as a fine for nonparticipation.
Though the Moravians had earnestly taught their boys to
be nonresistant, they feared that most of their "young
brethren would rather drill than pay so much money." An
older brother then spoke to them one at a time, pointing
out to them that military affairs were no part of their life
as Christians, and that it would thus be better to "free
ourselves with money" from the obligation of drilling,
"which might result in injury to our souls."

   The Mennonites, Amish, and Brethren did not see the
"contribution" or fine or tax in quite the same light.
Bishop Benjamin Hershey and two other Mennonite men
attended a meeting of representatives of the three denominations with the Lancaster Committee of Correspondence, where they informed the committee that
the present arrangement was not working in their
"societies." As long as the requirements or fines were
requested on a voluntary basis, there would be members
who would not contribute. The nonresistant leaders were
thinking, in fact, of approaching the Continental
Congress itself, to lay their beliefs before that body. In
the Franconia area to the east the ministers were almost
unanimously of the opinion that the Mennonites "should
not pay this tax to the government, considering it rebellious and hostile to the King." It was indeed most confusing to contemplate the shifting structures of civil au-

thority. The king himself was shortly to proclaim all the
Colonies in a state of rebellion. Out of nowhere, seem-
ingly, had mushroomed Committees of Correspondence,
of Observation, and of Safety, sometimes overlapping in
their informally defined roles, and none of them elected
under the Pennsylvania charter given by Penn which had
been prized almost as an article of faith by the Mennonites. The regular provincial Assembly was constantly
being bypassed by the rump Continental Congress. The
military associations had their own rules, and the captains
they elected often made loud demands on their
unassociated neighbors. Who was the Caesar to whom the
defenseless Christians should render tribute?

There was actually one important exception to the
unanimity of the Franconia Mennonites, prosperous
Bishop Christian Funk, now in his mid-forties. In his
opinion the defenseless Mennonites could appropriately
pay the three pounds ten shillings, thus acknowledging
the authority of the new political arrangement, because,
as he put it, they had already taken the money issued
under the authority of Congress, and paid their debts
with it. For the time being Christian's individualistic
opinion on this matter caused no difficulty. The bitterness of associators toward those who neither drilled nor
paid had not yet peaked. Mennonites were allowed to live
quietly, ignoring their neighbors' warlike opinions for the
most part, and so the issue did not become inflamed immediately.

But it remained pressing. The Pennsylvania Assembly
resolved to earnestly recommend to the associators that
they not abuse the conscientious, who were in turn asked,
in proportion to their means, to assist "chearfully" their

neighbors who had extra expense through military obliga-tions. The Assembly's advice, which was carefully considered by Benjamin Hershey, was repeated within a few weeks by the larger Continental Congress, also meet-ing in Philadelphia. This body acknowledged that there existed in the Colonies people who, "from religious prin-ciples, cannot bear arms in any case." Congress wished it to be clear that it intended no violence to their consciences, although it also earnestly recommended, as had the Assembly, that such people "contribute liberally . . . to the relief of their distressed brethren," as in Massachusetts.

Still using the language of voluntary cooperation, the Congress went on to "recommend," on July 18, 1775, that all able-bodied men throughout the Colonies should form themselves into companies of militia, each selecting a captain, two lieutenants, an ensign (flag-carrier), a drummer, and a fifer. Every soldier was to have a musket with a bayonet, a steel ramrod, a worm for extracting a wad or ball from the muzzle of a gun, priming wire, brush, cartridge box, twelve flints, sword or tomahawk, and a knapsack. Gunmakers were to be encouraged throughout "the united Colonies." Committees of Safety were to be appointed to keep order, now that former legal structures were becoming moribund. A day of fasting and prayer was to be kept.

Pious people, whether Moravian, Lutheran, or Men-nonite, grew ever more deeply perplexed and sadly amazed. The Moravians at Lititz prayed for their country on the fast day, but also "for George III our king" and his government. Pastor Helmuth of the Lutheran Church in Lancaster could not determine, as he put it, whether

America was doing right or wrong. The people about him were "all in a veritable enthusiasm regarding freedom." Even school pupils, as he had observed in Philadelphia, "are organized in soldier companies, wear their uniforms, and are drilled like regular troops. What the father does, the child simply imitates." Many preachers depict "those who have been killed on the American side . . .as martyrs." If only, Pastor Helmuth mused, "the human race were for once as zealous and unanimous in asserting their spiritual freedom as they now are here in America in respect to bodily freedom!"

Wherever large communities of nonresistants lived military officials complained. In York it was found that "those People equally scruple subscribing as bearing arms." The officers spoke of the glaring impropriety of one part of the community needing to defend the whole, including those who "won't so much as touch" the responsibility "with their little finger." James Smith suggested to the Continental Congress that if a regular tax would be laid on them by official act, it would be paid without trouble, since it was a religious principle of such groups to pay duly levied tribute uncomplainingly. In Berks County 152 pounds was raised by "divers Inhabitants" who would not bear arms and given to the County Committee of Safety. In Bucks County, where many Quakers lived, supplemented by the easternmost settlement of Mennonites with names like Wismer, Gross, Fretz, and Stover, the astonishing fact was that nearly half of the male population were non-associators, as of September 1775. Here and in Lancaster County many Mennonite families now had their guns confiscated.

During the fall of 1775 a series of petitions from

military associations were presented to the Pennsylvania Assembly, requesting that the pacifists be required by "some decisive plan" to contribute toward the general cause. Too many people were making conscience a convenience, in the opinion of the militia officers. Benjamin Franklin himself requested that some plan be devised. Those who could not because of conscience make a military contribution, should make "a pecuniary one" based on a fixed rate of assessment, he argued. If the benefits of the struggle against the British are universal, "it is not consonant to justice or equity that the burden should be partial," Franklin wrote.

As always, Franklin could state his opinions with disarming diplomacy, seeming to defend the very virtues his readers cherished. In comparison, the simple "Dutch" Mennonites would seem tonguetied and stupid. Yet they held other assumptions about reality, about the will of God. These Franklin, in his suave sentences that seemed so rational, disclaimed on the basis, ultimately, of the reality of force. He would not engage the nonresistants on the grounds where they stood, simply because such grounds seemed to him visionary at best, stupidly and dangerously pietistic at worst. For all his accents of reason, Franklin stood with his own logic backed by powder and shot. On the day he recommended pecuniary collections from pacifists, he also called for the construction of a magazine to store ammunition in Philadelphia.

No one was more gifted in mechanical ability than astronomer David Rittenhouse, and so he was appointed the chief engineer of Pennsylvania's military machine. The name that had been associated for generations with weaponlessness now was identified with the casting of cannon from iron and brass, experimenting with rifling cannon and muskets, manufacturing saltpeter, and finding a way to stretch a huge chain of logs across the Delaware to keep British ships out of the Philadelphia harbor. As Rittenhouse turned his attention to these projects, General George Washington was beginning to recruit a continental army to supplement the troops of which he had taken command four months earlier on the outskirts of Boston.

Supplies were now shipped up to Massachusetts from the unblockaded Middle Colonies, which required the impressment of a great many farm wagons and teams of horses. Many families, including Mennonites, were deeply concerned that their horses be returned in good condition after their tour of duty. Thus Abraham Wismer, Abraham Fretz, and Jacob Stover, all young men of the Mennonite community near Deep Run in Bucks County, were sent along with the family horses and wagons to bring them back in good shape. Fretz, it was claimed, put on a load of powder at Trenton and drove it all the way to Boston. Stover was said to have been in such service for a longer period, having once tried unsuccessfully to escape. Later his family would claim that he hauled, on occasion, the personal effects of Washington himself. Such cooperation with the military was tolerated among Mennonite and Schwenkfelder young men because their families felt that they were only taking care of their own property, which had been officially seized for a time by the authorities, and because the young men were not yet members of the church.

As the winter of 1775 approached, Quakers, Mennonites, and Brethren sensed the need to clarify their beliefs to the Pennsylvania Assembly, which was itself increasingly under pressure from radicals to take money from non-associators and give it to those who would take up arms. The Friends' Meeting for Sufferings filed a petition recalling their original reasons for coming to Pennsylvania and the guarantees of religious liberty they had received from William Penn. A "Committee of Philadelphia Patriots" quickly condemned this testimony, stating that "these gentlemen want to withdraw their persons and their fortunes from the service of their country at a time when their country stands most in need of them." Once again the assumptions regarding "country" were in disagreement. Those who were ready to make their conception of country stick with the backing of tar and feathers first and by rifle if need be, claimed the backing of logic and religion as well.

On his farm just west of near Lancaster, the seventy-eight year old Bishop Benjamin Hershey was also composing on behalf of Mennonites and Brethren a statement for the Assembly. Written in German, translated into English, and signed by ministers of both groups, it was presented to the House, now hardly able to function, on November 7, 1775. Benjamin titled it, "A Short and Sincere Declaration, To our Honorable Assembly," as well as to all other interested persons.

Benjamin begins by acknowledging the goodness and love of the most high God, revealed to mankind in Jesus Christ, who has been given all power in heaven and on earth. Further, he wishes to "heartily thank" the Assembly for continuing to allow the jewel of "liberty of conscience" to those who cannot bear arms. Every favor and "lenity" the Assembly may show toward the least of

Christ's brethren, among whom, writes the bishop, the defenseless Christians "by His grace hope to be ranked," will not be forgotten at the day of judgment.

With simple words the elderly bishop then places before the lawmakers of his province the essential Mennonite beliefs about war, going beyond the biblical doctrine to the divine heart of love in the nature of the Christ he follows. We receive with "chearfulness," he observes, the Assembly's advice to aid those who are distressed, "it being our principle to feed the hungry and give the thirsty drink." Further, "We have dedicated ourselves to serve all Men in every Thing that can be helpful to the Preservation of Men's Lives, but we find no Freedom in giving, or doing, or assisting in any Thing by which Men's Lives are destroyed or hurt. We beg the Patience of all those who believe we err in this Point."

As in the petition to the same body which he had signed two decades earlier, Benjamin reiterates the thanks of his people for a benevolent government, while humbly stating the utter impossibility of taking up arms "to conquer our enemies." Mennonites will rather, he writes, "pray to God, who has Power in Heaven and on Earth, for *us* and *them*." Regarding temporal citizenship, "We are always ready . . . to pay Taxes, and to render unto Caesar those Things that are Caesar's and to God those Things that are God's." The Old Swiss teaching on "*Niedrichkeit*"—lowliness—is expressed in the bishop's remark that, though we render worship to God, "we think ourselves very weak to give God his due Honor, He being a Spirit and Life, and we only Dust and Ashes."

Thus a testimony that had begun 250 years earlier in Zurich was now kept clear before an emerging govern-

ment in the quarrelsome New World. The response of the
legislature, now about to be replaced by a revolutionary
body, was to make things tougher for the pacifists. The
Assembly appointed a committee to replace the un-
dependable "contributions" of the non-associators with
regular taxes. Two weeks later the House asked for a careful accounting of the contributions handed in thus far by
the "Menonists, Omish Menonists, and Sunday-Baptists
in Lancaster County," and of how much of these
contributions had already been paid out "for the use of
any and what battalions or company" of militia in
Lancaster County.

The screws were now to be turned more tightly on
tender consciences. Whether or not defenseless Christians wished to fight, their money was to be used to pay
those who would, and to buy them ammunition. Ben
Franklin and David Rittenhouse called that making the
burden of "liberty" equal. Andrew Ziegler of Lower Salford saw it as forcing nonresistant people to go to war.

Chapter 5

Independence!

For Bishop Andrew Ziegler, now approaching the age of seventy, the great issue of the times was simple: Americans were in unlawful rebellion against their king. The Bible clearly taught that Christians must honor and pay required tribute to the powers that be. In the very first public statement the Mennonites had issued to their English neighbors in Pennsylvania in 1727, Andrew's father Michael, David Rittenhouse's grandfather Claus, and the young Benjamin Hershey of Lancaster had signed their names beneath an expression of readiness "to pay all required Taxes, Tolls, Excises and convoy Charges, truly and willingly, without deficiency." Of course Mennonites had always been prepared to refuse to obey when Caesar claimed the right to force their consciences to take an oath, or kill, or baptize babies.

But what were Americans doing now? They were refusing to pay taxes because, they said, they had not been involved in the decisions which instituted the taxes. Was this conscience or covetousness? The king, to keep his authority from being undermined, had put teeth into the laws, and to this the Americans had reacted with naked force. If this was not rebellion, Andrew did not know what it was.

For himself, he had no grievances against the king. As a German, he found tea an unemotional topic. The quarrel was someone else's, not his. Who could complain about the exceptional freedom that had been arranged for Pennsylvania by its Quaker founder so that saddler Andrew was at liberty to make his living, market his family's produce in Philadelphia, administrate the wills of his neighbors, and worship unmolested in the simple meetinghouses scattered among the quiet farming bottoms of the Colony? Was not this an amazing, unprecedented improvement over the situation on the European Continent? Who were these agitators who wrote in the papers, often without signing their names, and rode about delivering harangues and fanning the flames of hatred against Britain? As though the king rather than our own human nature were the source of all our troubles!

Why, rather than pay a small tax on tea, must there now be amassing on the heights overlooking Boston an illegal army ready to cannonade the town and drive the king's soldiers into the sea? Why could not friendly negotiations, however difficult, be continued? Many good people preferred this method. Was it not immeasurably more expensive to settle the feud by raising a congress as well as an army, manufacturing munitions, and taking apprentices away from productive work to drill, shoot, and drink? And then, to pay for it all by printing illegal money that was already inflating spectacularly, forcing everybody who used it to help pay for the war? Was paying taxes laid by Parliament, though they might be ill-advised and burdensome, really "abject slavery," "intolerable," "servile"? By whose standards, and why should they be forced on everyone?

In townships like Andrew's, the people who were quickest to leave shop or plow to follow the drum were often those with the least stake in the settled life of the community. As patriot David Rittenhouse himself wrote, the Associators were "chiefly composed" of "the Class of Men, who live from day to day on the products of their Industry—Mechanicks, Tenants & Laborers." Their motives did not impress Mennonites like Andrew Ziegler favorably. For that matter, many other country people despised the sound of the recruiter's drum along their roads with equal vehemence. Such disgust received expression one day in November of 1775 when a group of soldiers bringing enlistees to Philadelphia along the "Lancaster Road," stopped to refresh themselves at a wayside inn owned by a Mr. Musser.

A young unenlisted lad, whom the recruiters had met, marched with them to the tavern. During their pause they invited him to enlist, and he immediately seemed willing. The innkeeper and a doctor who happened to be present told the soldiers they had no business enlisting the boy, since he was an apprentice in the neighborhood. The drummer asked for proof, stating that if he was convinced of this, he would let the young fellow alone. The doctor flew into a rage, calling the recruiters "a parcel of Vagabonds and Rebels." Nobody "but Blackguards," he spat out, "would enlist," and struck the drummer in the face. A battle royal ensued, with the unarmed soldiers and their new recruits making for a nearby woods. Shortly the whole neighborhood was aroused, and "50 or 60 Men armed with Swords Pistols & Clubs" swarmed into the woods, surrounded, and beat up the soldiers, and marched them off down the road, prodding the slowest one with the sharp point of a sword until he had to be carried.

Even those who favored the organization of a militia were often contemptuous of the recruiting methods and bounties used. From the hill above his saddler's shop Andrew Ziegler could look north to the next ridge, just behind which stood the genteel double-brick mansion and tannery of Daniel Hiester, son-in-law of the Hager family for whom the town of Hagerstown, Maryland, would be named. Although Daniel himself was to be appointed colonel of the militia in Andrew Ziegler's district, it was with dismay that he watched his young brother-in-law, Jonathan Hager, Jr., walk up to a recruiting party in the nearby village of Sumneytown, where he had heard the drum beating near the tavern. Lieutenant Wirt, the recruiting officer, expressed considerable pleasure on seeing young Hager, whom he had once met briefly in Philadelphia, and who obviously represented a local family of some standing. The officer stated that he was enlisting riflemen, and asked Hager if he happened to have a good rifle. When the young gentleman said that he did, the lieutenant invited himself over to the Hiesters' to see the gun, and the older brother-in-law felt compelled by "civility" to invite him for breakfast.

After the meal on the following morning, the recruiting officer asked the young Hager to "step over with him a little" across the Unami Creek to Sumneytown. Nervously, the host asked his young brother-in-law to be sure

to come home again at once, and received his promise.
But once he had left, the boy was talked into going off
with the other recruits. Daniel Hiester was angry and
alarmed, and rode after the party until he caught up with
them at an auction nearly twenty miles away. There he
was met with insults and barely escaped without injury.
"And this," Bishop Andrew Ziegler may well have
mused, "is the kind of people who are fighting for our
liberty."

Unfortunately for those of Andrew's conservative position, King George III seemed perversely bent on making
nonviolent negotiation impossible. Even though the Congress had sent him an "Olive Branch" proposal regis-
tering their complaints but accepting his rule, he refused
even to receive it. Now the news reached Philadelphia
that 20,000 troops were being sent to subdue—and live
off—the Colonies. Many of these were said to be paid or
mercenary soldiers from German lands, since the average
British candidate for the army had little if any enthusiasm
for this war against his fellow citizens. By the end of 1775
it was fairly apparent, as Lutheran Pastor Muhlenberg of
Providence wrote, "that the flames of war will spread . . .
unless the Lord God, the supreme Ruler, determines
otherwise."

A few weeks later a bombshell, not of metal but of
words, exploded over the Colonies and set the minds of
Americans ablaze. Benjamin Rush, a well-known doctor
of Philadelphia, had asked a recent immigrant from England, a failed corset-maker and writer, to try publishing a
pamphlet arguing for a complete and final separation of
the Colonies from England. Dr. Rush felt it might be too
difficult for him to publish something like this himself,

connected as he was with many Philadelphians who were hostile to such an idea. Young Thomas Paine began to write, bringing his essay to Dr. Rush chapter by chapter for review. The physician was charmed by the forthrightness and crispness of Paine's arguments, especially with the sentence, "Nothing can be conceived of more absurd than three millions of people flocking to the American shore every time a vessel arrives from England, to know what portion of liberty they shall enjoy." Dr. Rush told his new friend to show the essay to Ben Franklin, Sam Adams, and David Rittenhouse, whom he knew to be "decided friends to American independence." When Paine asked about a title, the doctor suggested simply, "Common Sense," and it appeared thus in the *Pennsylvania Gazette.*

Never in American history, before or after, has a document so electrified the populace. Paine estimated that 120,000 of the pamphlets were sold within three months. George Washington remarked that he found the essay to be "working a powerful change in the minds of men." Paine's method was to simplify the issue and state it with sarcastic passion, appealing to "the simple voice of nature and reason," and, where useful, to reverence for the will of "the Almighty." For him it was as clear that it was morally wrong as well as stupid to obey a fatuous king, as it was certain to Andrew Ziegler that it was immoral to disobey.

Who are kings, after all? asked Paine. If we could trace back through history, "we should find the first of them nothing better than the principal ruffian of some restless gang, whose savage manners . . . obtained him the title of chief among plunderers." Looking at William the Con-

queror, the forerunner of the present line of British
royalty, Paine observed saltily, "A French bastard, land-
ing with an armed banditti and establishing himself king
of England against the consent of the natives, is in plain
terms a very paltry rascally original. It certainly hath no
divinity in it."

One by one Paine set up the traditional arguments for
loyalty to George III, in order to demolish them contemp-
tuously. America no longer needs a parent country, especially one that devours its own young, unlike even animals and savages. Our connection with England only
forces us to participate in her wars against nations with
whom we ourselves have no quarrel. "Everything that is
right or reasonable pleads for separation. The blood of the
slain, the weeping voice of nature cries, *'Tis time to
part.*' "

As if to reinforce the futility of trying to keep the tie
with Britain, the word arrived a few weeks after *Common
Sense* had appeared that the Colonies were now removed
from the protection of the Crown, and all American ships
at sea were to be seized. The momentum toward an
outright declaration of independence began to build in
Congress. The patriotic spirit shooting out from
Philadelphia caught fire afresh in distant settlements.

Although Father Muhlenberg continued to remain
aloof from what he considered a political clash, one of his
sons, a pastor in a group of small Lutheran congregations
in the Shenandoah Valley of Virginia, made up his mind
quickly. "I am a clergyman, it is true," he wrote, "but I
am a member of society as well, and my liberty is as dear
to me as any man. . . . I am called by my country in its defence; the cause is just and noble. Were I a bishop, even a

Lutheran one, I should obey without hesitation. . . . I am
convinced it is . . . a duty I owe to my God and to my
country."

For over two centuries the story would be told that on
Sunday morning, January 21, 1776, Pastor John Peter
Gabriel Muhlenberg, already a member of his country's
Committee of Safety and commissioned as colonel of the
Eighth Virginia Regiment, gave his congregation at
Woodstock a shock. He had been preaching on the third
chapter of Ecclesiastes, which states that there is a proper
time for everything. Culminating his peroration with the
words, "There is a time to fight!" he threw back his robe,
revealing the uniform of a military officer. On the spot he
enlisted most of the able-bodied men of his congregation,
and went on to become one of the leading generals in
Washington's army.

Heartened by news that Washington had maneuvered
General Howe into evacuating his troops from Boston,
Congress exhorted all the Colonies to create "such
government as shall best conduce to the happiness and
safety of their constituents." The recruiting of 13,500
more militiamen from the Middle Colonies for Washington's army was authorized. All over the countryside
citizens prepared to fight, or remained, as the Moravians
of Lititz resolved to remain, "absolutely inactive."
Benjamin Rittenhouse, mechanically gifted brother of
David, drilled the company of militia over which he was
captain in Norriton Township, and was requested by the
Philadelphia Committee of Safety to "establish a Gun
Lock Manufactory, with a view that a great number of
hands may be immediately employed." And in distant
North Carolina, Abel Kolb, a cousin of Andrew Ziegler's

wife, was elected captain of the local militia. Though, like his Mennonite ancestors, he was of a "retiring disposition," his resourcefulness made him a leader among the Baptists among which he had now settled and married. Eventually he was to be killed in an attack by local Loyalists embittered by the success of the Revolution.

For months there was suspense, in the spring of 1776, regarding where General Howe might land his British troops, which he had taken from Boston to Nova Scotia. The question was answered at the end of June when he appeared in New York Harbor, and landed 10,000 men on Staten Island. The British strategy was to send troops up the Hudson River Valley to meet others coming down from Lake Champlain, and thus divide rebellious New England from its source of supplies in the Middle Colonies. General Washington, who by now had trained an army of about 16,000 men, was waiting with them nearby. He believed that "the safety of America" depended on keeping the way open between Pennsylvania and New England. Lord Howe's reinforcements continued to arrive, including 8,000 Hessian mercenaries, until his forces totaled 32,000 professional soldiers.

As both sides prepared for battle, guns were collected throughout the Colonies, particularly from non-associators—Mennonites, Moravians, and Quakers. In Bucks County the committee leader, Henry Wynkoop, received thirty-nine guns for his forces from Rockhill, and thirteen from Bedminster. The report was brought back that some persons had refused to surrender arms in their possession, and a resolution was passed by the local committee authorizing collectors to call on the militia for enforcement. One Mennonite farmer in his mid-forties who was unhappy to see the collectors visit his home was John Fretz. When the men asked for his gun he took it from its usual place, according to family tradition, and said to the soldiers, "You can have my gun, but I'll keep hold of the butt end." The descendants of John, who emigrated to Canada after the War and served as the first Mennonite deacon there, would not include in their story an account of who won this argument.

A clash of arms was now imminent, and the old Pennsylvania Assembly, confused and betwixt, adjourned what was to be its last working session. Four days later a call went out from Carpenters' Hall in Philadelphia, where the Committee of Observation from the province had met, for a "new government in the authority of the people only." The support of Pennsylvania's citizens for this move was not unanimous. Many considered the creation of a new government a breaking of their promise of loyalty to the king, given at their naturalization as Pennsylvania citizens.

Thirty miles north, along the Indian Creek in Franconia Township, miller-bishop Christian Funk decided that for once he would attend a township meeting. It had been announced that Franconia should elect three men to attend the convention in Philadelphia which should deliberate the issues of independence for the colony of Pennsylvania. Christian was worried that the special liberties of the Penn charter might be endangered, once it was obrogated and another basic of law brought in. When he arrived at the meeting, he found that intense interest had convened nearly the whole township. Two thirds of the gathering, by his estimate, were Mennonites, including his uncle, Deacon Christian Meyer,

and two other recently ordained farmers from along In-
dian Creek, Deacon Henry Rosenberger and Minister
Jacob Oberholtzer. The crowd was composed entirely of
German-speaking   men,   mingling   Lutheran   and
Reformed people with Mennonites and a few Brethren.
The non-Mennonites, referred to as "church people," as
opposed to those who went to "meeting (*Versammlung*),
included a number of military enthusiasts.

Bishop Funk, the wealthiest man in the township,
asked whether any decision had been made before he had
arrived. When he found that the issue was still open, he
expressed his opinion. "Defenseless people," he told his
largely Mennonite audience, could neither "institute nor
destroy any government." The king, to whom they had
given their word of loyalty, was the rightful "head or pro-
tector of Pennsylvania," and it was therefore necessary to
submit to his authority, even to the three "intolerable"
acts which had so inflamed public opinion. It was thus obvious, said the bishop, that the Mennonites "could not interfere in tearing ourselves from the King."

With these sentiments his brethren all agreed, but their
views were not to be honored by history, or at least those
who would write it. On July 2 the Continental Congress
voted to declare independence, and on the fourth
adopted a declaration to that effect written primarily by
Thomas Jefferson. A week later the newspapers had carried the news to the Lititz Moravian community. "Independence was actually declared by Congress," wrote
their diarist, "and all the provinces made free states. God
help us!"

Chapter 6

A New Constitution—and an
Army!—in Penn's Woods

The first month of American independence was the last of the earthly life of Strong Isaac Kolb, brother-in-law of Andrew Ziegler, and fellow bishop with him and Christian Funk. He died just in time to miss the invasion of Revolutionary polarization in the councils of his church.

Throughout the Colonies, this "party-spirit" was dividing families, occasionally running along generational lines. Whereas Andrew Ziegler and Christian Meyer, who had both reached seventy, were appalled at the revolutionary actions of the Congress, their colleague Christian Funk, in his mid-forties, found himself becoming willing to consider the changes as less than totally evil. This shocked his fellow ministers and, for the first time since he had been ordained, Christian detected a note of estrangement in their relationship. Possibly their critical attitude was merely their jealous response to the economic success of the aggressive Funk family.

The air was filled with distrust, and discontent was universal in the community, Christian observed. It even

led to "mutual abuse" among former friends. Out at
Lititz the Moravian community was warned by its leaders
that two parties had now come to exist, "not only among
the brethren but also in the congregation; the one party
for the king, which they name Tories, and the other the
Whigs, which upholds the present government." This
could not be acceptable to God, admonished the leaders.
Both those who shamefully slandered the king and those
who spoke and acted in opposition to the present government, they said, were failing to wait solely on the will of
God, which was the proper course. Emphatically but
kindly the older boys were warned that they were taking
too much interest in the war and the state of the country
for the good of the community.

It was certainly impossible, in the summer of 1776, not
to be affected by the news of changes in the government
and military maneuvers. The new Pennsylvania Convention, under the leadership of the elderly but still vigorous
and overworked Benjamin Franklin, was writing a
Constitution—the first in the Colonies. A Council of
Safety was set up to run the affairs of the province during
the transition of government. In this body David Rittenhouse played a conspicuous role, along with the
nonpacifist Quaker Timothy Matlack. One of the early
steps taken by the Council was to order the officers of the
militia to take all the arms in the hands of non-associators
throughout Pennsylvania and, having given the owners
proper receipts, to turn these guns over to the militia. A
man who had worked as a mason for the Lititz Moravians
during the summer now came back as a militia lieutenant,
and announced that the able-bodied men of the community would be required to drill, or provide substitutes.

The leaders of the church then exhorted those whose names were read off in the various militia classes "to keep their word not to go to war, nor to furnish a substitute." They were admonished to "let matters take their course, and see what they can do to us."

Had there been no actual fighting between American and British troops, the growing pressure on non-associators would have doubtless lifted without any concrete confrontations. But on August 26 General Washington's army was surprised by a huge force of Redcoats on Long Island, and driven back in panic to Brooklyn. Among the 1,500 casualties suffered by the Americans was the slain brother-in-law of David Rittenhouse, and the captured Jonathan Hager, Jr., who had disappointed his own brother-in-law, Daniel Hiester, by enlisting at Sumneytown in the previous spring. It was a severe defeat, and the Revolutionary leaders were so discouraged that Benjamin Franklin, John Adams, and a third official were sent to meet the British General, Lord Howe, on Staten Island for peace negotiations. It looked to some Americans as though the war was about to end. The aristocratic Howe, however, laid down a condition the Americans would not accept: no peace negotiations until the Declaration of Independence was revoked. When Washington learned that the conference had fallen apart, he began to retreat, and a series of British raids lost him his command of the city of New York. With the British in control, a great conflagration burst out and destroyed much of the town.

New York being the second largest city in the Colonies, these events were extremely disheartening to the Revolutionaries in the new Colonial capital of Philadelphia, and tempers began to rise. More and more irritation was expressed over the failure of non-associators to carry their weight in the war—a war in which, of course, many of them did not believe, but which, they were warmly informed by Whigs, was their war too.

The Lititz Moravians were visited by a constable who read off a list of their able-bodied men, from each of whom, he promised, he would collect three pounds ten shillings when he returned in thirty days, as a fine for non-association. About three weeks later, just as the community sat down to dinner, a half dozen armed militiamen walked into the house, read off the names of nine single men, placed them under guard, and marched them five miles off to the village of Manheim, where they spent the night, still under guard, in the house of a militia captain. The next day, to the accompaniment of fife and drum, they were marched in Lancaster through a dense crowd of people yelling "Tory," to the Quaker Meeting House, and locked up there with a collection of other non-associators. The room was packed so full of bodies that they could neither sit nor lie down. Moravians of Lancaster than appealed to the Committee of the City , who immediately revoked the unwarranted arrests of the irascible militia captains and dismissed the prisoners "very kindly and politely," telling them that they needed henceforth to "listen to no one without he came express from them."

No such dramatic event stirred the peace of Franconia Township, where Christian Funk and his neighbor Jacob Oberholtzer preached among the Mennonites. But Jacob, whose farmhouse was the next dwelling up Indian Creek from Christian's mill, was unhappy with his fellow preacher's manners. He felt that Christian was too high and mighty, and that he did not sufficiently instruct his children to have a humble, cooperative spirit in their communal relations. It was true that Christian and two of his three brothers had seemed to prosper unusually. Abraham, who had sold the home mill to Christian and moved north to another home on Durham Creek in Bucks County, had become a leading businessman in his community. Henry, the oldest of the brothers, had bought a fine mill too, in the Hosensack Valley to the northwest, in a predominantly Schwenkfelder settlement. Here he had been ordained as a minister, but in a few years had been silenced by his colleagues for being too domineering.

Whether or not Jacob Oberholtzer was justified in his dissatisfaction with the vigorous miller on the next plantation who occupied the pulpit with him at the nearby Indianfield meetinghouse, there were others who shared it, including the bishop's elderly uncle, Deacon Christian Meyer. Their adjoining farms and the close intermarriage of their families kept each person's activities constantly visible to the others. A younger deacon, Henry Rosenberger, lived next to Minister Oberholtzer, and had given land for a burial plot next to the meetinghouse, which had previously been built on land donated by Deacon Meyer.

Bishop Funk, whose father had been an author, was more likely to be informed regarding events on the wider scene, and he managed to secure a copy of the new Constitution of Pennsylvania, which had been adopted on September 28, 1776. Having heard his neighbors' negative views of the upstart government, he was more than pleasantly surprised to find that the special "liberty

of conscience" granted by Penn was guaranteed afresh in
the new document. Wedded to Penn's generosity of spirit
were new concepts of natural rights, including that of the
people to change or abolish their government by due
process of law.

Although the Constitution had been hurriedly written
and pushed through to adoption without allowing the
citizens to vote on it, the tone was essentially benevolent
and liberal. There was an eloquent "Declaration of
Rights," largely influenced by Benjamin Franklin, which
stated that "every member of society hath a right to be
protected in the enjoyment of life, liberty and property,"
and that this right was based on his being "bound to
contribute his proportion toward the extent of that protection, and yield his personal service when necessary, or
an equivalent thereto." However, no "man who is conscientiously scrupulous of bearing arms" could be "justly
compelled thereto if he will pay such equivalent."

This, Christian Funk decided, was much better than he
had feared it might be. It was, in fact, acceptable to
defenseless Christians, since, as he argued, no one would
be "compelled to bear arms, or to take an oath against his
conscience." How can we, he asked, despise the government that offers "us the like liberty which William Penn
had guaranteed to our fathers in Europe?"

Here Christian and the other writers of the Declaration
of Rights were not fully leveling with the objections of the
religious non-associators. The very requirement of a
"contribution" to the war effort "equivalent" to military
service, whether in money or goods, was something
William Penn would never have approved (though he
was in favor, for instance, of capital punishment), and it

weighed heavily on the consciences of most of the defenseless Mennonites. Christian's fellow ministers were united in their opinion of the new government, especially the Congress, as rebellious, and they sharply disapproved of Whig sentiments.

The publishing of the Constitution divided the populace into Loyalists and Whigs, with perhaps a third of the people opposing the legitimacy of the Revolutionary government. Many could not forget that they had, in a recent decade, given their solemn word of loyalty to the king, and the Mennonites, who had refused to give an oath, nevertheless considered their word to be their bond. Some thought, in fact, that they could not expect God's grace to save them if they broke their word, and thus dishonored their covenant with God.

With considerable caution, Christian Funk now began to broach the thought, among his congregation, "that we ought not to denounce the American government as *rebellious*." Already there existed "four republics"—countries without kings—and "perhaps America might become another." Let the Americans and the British fight it out without prejudging the outcome, and without teaching our people not to trust the new government, he advised. Who knows which side, in the providence of God, will win? After all, "the English had taken America from the Spaniards; and the Americans were about to wrest it from them." Had not the Mennonite farmers along Indian Creek accepted deeds to their land from a government that had taken it from the Indian natives at a pitifully small price so that now only the last of the "Original People"—the Lenni Lenape—remained forlornly on the farms of **Minister Jacob Shoemaker** of

Skippack and his son Michael of Franconia?

But such reasoning was, in the eyes of Christian Funk's brethren, "foolishness." Besides, he was not ordering his family acceptably, and he was becoming too high-minded. He was taking too much interest in the affairs of the world, and forgetting the admonition the Mennonites had published to the world in 1727, borrowing from an earlier Dutch writer, that "it behoves and becomes a right and true Christian that he should be little and low in the World, and shun the greatness of the same, and keep himself like the lowly ones."

Doubtless Christian had read this statement, signed by his forefathers and offered to the world as an explanation of the "supposed newness" of the defenseless doctrine. Doubtless too, he had read in it allusions to the "discord" or "breach" in the Dutch Mennonite fellowship over doctrinal issues. Perhaps, even, it was this that had motivated him in the letter to the Dutch of three years previous to ask them, with Isaac Kolb and Andrew Ziegler, whether the breach had been fully healed, and if not, whether the brethren could "bear themselves toward each other with love." Now, little as he suspected it, the divisiveness of the worldly Whig and Tory spirits was about to invade the quiet conversations of his congregations.

The wheat and corn Christian ground in his mill that fall came of a weak harvest, which, with the steep inflation of Continental money, drove prices to alarming heights. "One hears complaints upon complaints," wrote Lutheran Pastor Muhlenberg, "over the dearness of things." Muhlenberg took a dim view of Quakers and other sects who "with their tender consciences . . . prefer to gather up and hoard crops rather than Continental

money." And in addition to this problem, the rich farms
of the Germans, especially those of non-associators, were
being visited with increasing frequency by foragers from
the army and militia, seeking horses and provender for
their companies. The small Mennonite community in the
Butter Valley at Hereford in Berks County was paid an
unwelcome call by hungry soldiers just as a household of
guests was sitting down to a wedding meal. It was at the
home of Michael Bauer, whose oldest daughter Fannie
had just been married to a young man named Christian
Meyer. As their descendants would tell it, the soldiers not
only "ate and ate the things away," but went outside and
caught as many turkeys and chickens as they could find,
and drove back to their camp with a wagonload of the
plunder.

Pennsylvania's farms were indeed a breadbasket for
Washington's growing but continuously defeated army,
still in the vicinity of New York. The Pennsylvania Militia
or "Flying Camp," which was supplementing his regular
Army, suffered heavy losses by capture when the British
took Fort Washington, just outside of New York City, on
November 16. These men had to be replaced by new
recruitments, but when Pennsylvania's Council of Safety,
under David Rittenhouse's leadership, addressed themselves to the assignment, they were angry. Soldiers must
be found, but there were so many conscientious non-
associators in Pennsylvania, many of whom would not
drill and had never yet been actually forced to pay an
"equivalent," be it three pounds ten shillings or
whatever, that the bottom was knocked out of the
recruiting system. "The situation of our Militia," fumed
Rittenhouse, "is a public Calamity." The soldiers have

been campaigning with Washington in New York, where they have suffered "Inconveniences, hardships and losses," Rittenhouse said, while the non-associators have been "permitted to remain at home in the peaceable enjoyment of their possessions," sometimes "grasping the trade of the Associators." Not only were the associators, for all their pains, often sneered at, but above all they had been wholly disappointed in "their just & reasonable expectations of seeing the nonassociators obliged to pay something for the indulgences which had been granted them." The voluntary contribution system had not worked. Many Mennonites had simply ignored it as an unwelcome demand of an upstart government.

From the Mennonite point of view, it was strange to have a regime appoint itself to power, require its citizens to do what they had been promised by the original government they would never have to do, and then speak of these requirements as "indulgences." Stranger still was it for the fiery war rhetoric that was closing the noose about their peaceable convictions to come from the mouth of the grandson of one of their defenseless ministers. Claus Rittenhouse of Germantown had endorsed, only forty-nine years earlier, the letter to the Pennsylvania public which expressed a traditional Mennonite amazement "that so many high gifted, and understanding and excellent men," who had "received Knowledge and clear shining Light of the Gospel," had "so little altered themselves" from the sub-Christian "Customs" of the world.

It had been "clear" to the famous astronomer's ancestors for two centuries, had, in fact, been "one of the weightiest Articles of our Doctrine and Religion, that without any Worldly Might or Fleshly Defence and Weapons, the Lord Christ must be preached and followed Revengeless." This was not in the least a result of contempt for good authority. It was simply that "we can understand nothing else out of the New Testament, but that the Lord Christ hath so learned, and with his own Example gone before us. . . ." If we live according to the example of Christ, our conduct will be "a great Light, worthy of the Christian Name, lighted and set upon the Candlestick." The basic content of this teaching is that we desire "to be hurtful to none, but to be profitable and helpful to all People." As a result these people had confessed, since 1524, that for them all killing had been abandoned.

Such words, endorsed by David Rittenhouse's grandfather, are the confessions of people who live at once in two kingdoms—their time-bound political arrangements, and the eternal kingdom of God, where love is willing to go to a cross rather than wreak revenge or set up the sword of defense. With their life's blood David Rittenhouse's Mennonite forebears had paid for their loyalty to this kingdom. But now, as an American statesman, he had taken up the language of a tradition which, while it contained enlightened aspects of the modern age, was wedded to the ancient belief that the sword must be the final arbiter in the most difficult human disputes. Heaven, in fact, in this conventional wisdom, delights in the defense of our earthly borders, and David describes his compatriots as "Men who ask the Blessing of God on their Endeavors," though they "leave Events to him who governs the Universe."

Thus, while the backward country Mennonites refuse

to involve themselves in a modern cause, their enlightened city cousin passionately depicts the "Chains, Desolation, violated Virgins, and abused Infants" which their supine unwillingness to fight will allow (without mentioning the fact that none of these things would be happening were it not for the Colonies' revolt). All this is to bolster the request that at long last a fine be levied "immediately on every able Bodied Man from the age of 16 to 50 years, who shall refuse or neglect to go into Service." Persons over the age of fifty should be reasonably assessed. Further, urges Rittenhouse, the collectors should be given the legal power to take the property of those who neither march nor pay, and "make sale thereof." The money thus realized should "be divided among those . . . in actual service as Militia."

Bishops Andrew Ziegler and Christian Funk would never see the letter in which Rittenhouse called for these taxes, but they and their congregations would shortly feel its weight. They would lack eloquence to answer the astronomer-patriot in the English language, had they so desired. One Tory voice in a Philadelphia newspaper did call the scientist back, not to his Mennonite heritage, but to his telescope:

TO DAVID RITTENHOUSE

Meddle not with State affairs,
Keep acquaintance with the Stars;
Science, David, is thy line;
Warp not Nature's great design,
If thou to fame wouldst rise.

Spurred by fears resulting from the continued British

victories, which by early December had Washington reel-
ing back across New Jersey into Pennsylvania with hardly
more than 3,000 men, the embarrassed legislature
responded to Rittenhouse's request by resolving unanimously to "take immediate measures to make effectual . . . the collection of fines" from non-associators,
and that it would "as soon as possible enact a Militia
Law" which would "put the defence of the State on a just
and equitable footing." Thus the grandson of a Mennonite had made the request, and a Quaker had recorded
the response of the government that would require their
conscientious relatives to pay the fruit of their labors to
support the military resolution of a cause they rejected.

Meanwhile, Philadelphia and the countryside around it
were filled with "much alarm . . . and great excitement"
by "the progress of the British army." Many Pennsylvanians welcomed the prospect of having the Revolutionary Army put out of business so that they could get
back to normal life. "It is said to the joy of many, and the
terror of many more," noted Pastor Muhlenberg, "that
the British Armies will eat their Christmas dinner in
Philadelphia." The Tories, of course, could think of nothing better. But while Washington's battered army tried to
pull itself together to head off this prospect, Thomas
Paine produced another essay as stingingly effective as
Common Sense had been eleven months earlier.
"These," he admitted proudly, "are the times that try
men's souls," and they have the advantage of showing
people in their true colors. "Ye men of Pennsylvania," he
appealed, "do reason upon these things." Why has
General Howe brought the war to the doorstep of Pennsylvania, but that he knows he will find more support

here? "New England is not infested with tories, and we are. . . . And what is a tory? Good God! what is he? . . . Every tory is a coward; for servile, slavish, self-interested fear is the foundation of toryism. . . ."

Having thus explained for the public the motives of those who would not voluntarily rise to support the Revolution, Paine predicted the results of not defeating the British: "a ravaged country—a depopulated city—our homes turned into barracks and bawdy houses for the Hessians, and a future race to provide for, whose fathers we shall doubt of. Look on this picture and weep over it!"

Considerably less lurid, but still a grave nuisance were the actual circumstances surrounding the approach of either American or British soldiers. One of the most ironic of the innumerable confiscations that took place throughout the war involved the unbound copies of the *Martyrs Mirror*, for which Christian Funk's father had read the proofs three decades earlier. Although perhaps 1,200 of the folio volumes (later claimed to have been the largest books published in the Colonies) had been printed at the Ephrata Cloister in Lancaster County, several hundred had remained unsold. When a half dozen soldiers arrived with two wagons, in search of paper for wadding muskets in the Continental Army, the Brothers of the Cloister where the unbound pages remained stored were said to have considered at first some form of resistance. But they ended by surrendering the paper, and doubtless even the title page, bearing the words, "The Bloody Drama of the Defenseless Christians" served to hold in place bullets which shed the blood of British and Hessian soldiers.

Foragers of both armies ranged through the communities on either side of the Delaware, taking food, guns, and horses from Whigs, Tories, and neutrals alike. Along nearby Tinicum Creek in Bucks County, an officer on horseback rode onto the farm of weaver Christian Fretz, brother of the John who refused to give up his gun. The officer had brought with him soldiers to carry hay back to the army, but noticed a fine horse in the barn. One of Christian's daughters heard the officer tell his men that he would try to buy the horse, and if that was not possible, would get it some other way. The girl ran into the house ahead of the officer, to tell her fifteen-year-old brother, Joseph, who owned the horse. As the officer came in the front door, Joseph left the loom where he had been weaving, jumped out a nearby window, took his horse from the barn, and rode westward toward heavily forested Haycock Mountain. The officer followed but soon lost him. Joseph pushed far into the unsettled woods, fording up streams to obliterate his tracks, and hid the horse.

Several days later the officer called at the Fretz farm again, insisting that he would have that horse. This was more than Joseph's father, a determined man who had once recovered a horse of his own which had been stolen by Indians, was ready to accept. The next day he went with a neighbor to the encampment of the American Army at Newtown, and requested the aid of a general who interviewed him. He was given a signed paper with instructions for the officer if he should come back. The officer did, and peremptorily demanded Joseph's horse. Christian Fretz handed him the paper. The officer read it, dropped it, and left.

Joseph kept his prized horse, as did farmer Christian Hunsberger of Franconia, who hid his among the boulders of Rock Hill, and the Salford farmers who reportedly piled corn shocks around their horses in the woods away from their barns. Still, many horses disappeared without a trace.

The excitement of approaching war varied with the distance from the Delaware. Colonel John Siegfried, innkeeper by the Lehigh River near the northernmost settlement of Mennonites, received instructions from Washington's Bucks County headquarters to bring down the militia of Northampton County to help Washington "put a stop to the purpose of the enemy who are making preparations to advance to Philadelphia." Siegfried's officers, among whom were some of the most persistent baiters of non-associators in the Colony, would now taste the war firsthand, and have their passions intensified.

And even as far away as Washington County in Maryland, where the Mennonites and Dunkers were granted the right to pay their militia fines in produce rather than money, there was fresh pressure to aid the war effort. An order was issued by the local Committee of Observation to the effect that those Dunkers and Mennonites who had still not enrolled should "immediately be requested to march with the Militia, in order to give their Assistance in intrenching and helping the sick. . . ." All who would respond voluntarily to the call would not be required to pay the fines. This offer was apparently not accepted, for on the day before Christmas the committee reported receiving fines of 206 pounds from the Dunkers and Mennonites who had refused to march.

On Christmas night, 1776, General Washington stunned the British by effecting an amazing, secret transfer of 2,400 men across the ice-floed Delaware River, marching them nine miles to Trenton in a snowstorm, and catching the Hessians napping. His 1,000 prisoners and captured ammunition were celebrated with whoops of joy throughout the patriot ranks, and the war suddenly looked less like a dying revolt, and more like the emergence of a new national power. For Washington, the trick was to hold his army together until the general populace would get more solidly behind him. If they thought the Revolution would succeed, many Americans would begin to believe in its logic. When Washington eluded a British counterattack and actually defeated them in a brief battle at Princeton, the Redcoats backed off, and Philadelphia was safe for the winter.

Chapter 7

Draft, Tax, and Test

As long as the war had remained at a distance, Pennsylvania's defenseless Christians had not been severely pressed by their "Presbyterian" neighbors to comply with the "recommendations" to enroll in the militia or contribute. But now that the British were threatening to bring the armed conflict toward the capital city of Philadelphia, stern measures were taken to make everyone declare his true political colors. One result was that Bishop Christian Funk was found to be shaded toward the Whig side. When he suggested that people who used the Continental money to do business might as well pay taxes and fines imposed by the government that issued the money, he was considered by his Mennonite neighbors to be reflecting an attitude deriving from "the world," not the brotherhood of the church. He was too quick to become interested in popular affairs, according to his neighbor, Minister Jacob Oberholtzer.

The trait of forwardness did seem to run in the Funk family. Christian's older brother, Henry, who had been ordained as a minister in the "Great Meadow" (Swamp) district soon after he had moved from Perkasie to Hosensack, had rapidly alienated his fellow-ministers there. Frequent quarrels erupted, with Henry's critics claiming that he was "too absolute" in his manner, and that he gave the impression of wanting the whole church to be subject to him. As a vigorous miller, he did a great deal of "public business," and was known as a "horse-swapper." Mennonites had a deeply ingrained tradition of disapproving of any occupation which required, or at least appeared to involve, any kind of sharpness in dealing, and they expected their ministers especially to abstain from all appearance of evil. When to these troublesome matters was added the report that Henry had not stuck to the truth in testifying before a local justice of the peace, the bishop of the Meadow district had silenced him, forbidding him to preach. Still, he remained a Mennonite, with many of his traditional nonresistant convictions, and acted as something of a community leader.

Neither Henry at Hosensack nor his brother Christian at Indian Creek experienced real trouble over the war issue itself until the Supreme Executive Council of Pennsylvania, stirred by rumors of the rapid approach of General Howe's army, passed two Acts that brought the issue of loyalty to a head. One created the first military draft in the history of Penn's Holy Experiment, and the other required an oath of allegiance. Both were considered absolutely necessary by a new government seeking to get a firm grip on a divided population, and both were fundamentally unfriendly to the special freedoms for which the Mennonites had migrated to Pennsylvania two generations earlier.

Oaths and drafts had not been able to weaken their mountain-farmer ancestors of Bern in Switzerland, where through centuries of persecution their harassed church had "flourished in spite of harassment." Their stubborn adherence to their despised, unofficial covenant-fellow-ship had become legendary. Though they had made no trouble outside of refusing to swear, fight, or have their babies baptized in the Reformed state church, they had been repeatedly jailed, fined, and exiled in vain attempts by officials to eradicate their fellowship without actual executions. They kept returning to the farms from which they had been banished, claiming that "the earth is the Lord's," and that thus no government had the right to remove a family from the land God had given. There were rights more ancient than those some educated gentlemen in the city had agreed to call law.

Their troubles reached a climax during the 1660s, soon after a special Commission for Anabaptist Affairs had been formed to suppress their fellowship. Though Dutch Mennonites and even the Dutch government protested against their methods, Bernese authorities imprisoned both men and women, whipping and branding, and threatening exile if their prisoners did not return to the state church. In 1666 two brothers and a sister of the Loetscher family had been jailed, with instructions from the Anabaptist Commission to local ministers to visit them and by strong teaching erase "their whims" from their young minds. Their toughness, however, had been underestimated. The brothers, Hans and Melchior, es-caped the prison in the following year, and after their re-capture were held for four years in a vain attempt to make them relent. Finally, in 1671, they were taken with four other Mennonite men in chains to Venice, and sentenced to toil as galley slaves. Even this did not break their will, and in 1673 they were apprehended once more in Bern, where they had returned to claim their father's estate.

While in jail this time, Hans Loetscher somehow got access to the prison record book, and copied out of it the names and sentences of some forty local Anabaptists who had been executed for their faith in the attempt to give the Reformed state church complete religious control of the countryside. This list was taken along by his relatives when finally, weary of harassment, they abandoned their native Switzerland in waves that led to the Palatinate, Holland, and Pennsylvania. A copy of it was handed in to the printers of the new Pennsylvania translation of the *Martyrs Mirror,* and thus the last additions to this vast Mennonite saga were set in type in the New World, and placed in the margins of the nearly completed volume.

The memory of their European struggles had not died among the Latschar's of Pennsylvania, grandchildren of Bernese farmers, by the time the jealousies of the American Revolution visited their peaceful community at Hereford, a few miles from Henry Funk's mill. They were prepared to resist once again with the stubbornness of their mountain-farmer forefathers. Abraham Latschar, thirty-eight-year-old father of eight, not only stated firmly that his conscience would not let him bear arms, but rode to a township meeting called for the purpose of organizing the local militia, and spoke his mind there. Colonel Daniel Hunter, he claimed, did not have governmental orders for this organization, and for that matter, the men who had set themselves up as the Assembly in Philadelphia "were no legal body."

This was extremely annoying to a local member of the Berks County Committee of Observation, who had just been appointed to the new Pennsylvania Council of Safety. Richard Tea, an ironmaster of Hereford, informed the Council that he could not leave home to take his seat among their body if there was not some improvement in the readying of a militia battalion that was supposed to be formed in his region. The influence of the people he called Tories was so strong that the battalion had never been able to muster fifty men at once. When Mr. Tea heard that Abraham Latschar had said at a tavern that he "would use me ill" if the gun that Mr. Tea had confiscated for the militia was not returned, he wrote to the Council, stating that without an improvement in the situation he would have to resign. He sent Abraham Latschar with five other men to answer for their behavior to the Council in person.

It was out of such complaints by officials seeking to enforce ill-defined, semi-voluntary "requirements" that the new, more ironclad legislation had emerged. The draft law came first, under the title, "An Act to Regulate the Militia of the Commonwealth of Pennsylvania." This divided each Pennsylvania County into eight "battalion" districts, which were in turn to raise eight companies of men each. Every company was to elect a captain and an ensign (flag-bearer). Companies were subdivided into eight "classes," not all of which would be asked to go on tours of duty at the same time. The colonel in charge of each battalion was to see that it was fully organized in six weeks from the date of the Act, and the first day the men would be required to muster for a drill was to be sooner than that—on April 21. Anyone on the roster (all able-

bodied men between eighteen and fifty-three) who did
not turn out for the exercise would be fined five shillings
for each day missed, and more for the days when the
whole battalion paraded.

Colonel for the First Battalion of Philadelphia County,
which included Franconia, Lower Salford, Towamencin,
and Skippack Townships, was the gentleman tanner
Daniel Hiester of Sumneytown. In Franconia the militia
company elected John Cope as captain; his Reformed
relatives were enthusiastic patriots, with his Lutheran
neighbors, but the bulk of Franconia was Mennonite, and
so his company tended to be thin. Those who did not
respond when the troops were called up for duty were
now legally required, as David Rittenhouse had wished,
to pay a substitute fine. It was no longer a "contribution"
but, in effect, a tax.

So many men in Lieutenant Colonel Hiester's battalion
turned out to be unwilling to drill or serve when called
(all eight companies saw duty in 1777), that by the end of
six months he had collected the astounding sum of nearly
10,000 pounds for substitute fines alone, and another 752
pounds in fines for missing exercise days. Thus the cost of
the war was now felt unmistakably by all families, and the
issue of whether to pay or not to pay became unavoidable.
Bishop Andrew Ziegler of Lower Salford Township was
vehemently opposed to paying, and in a visit to the region
near Abraham Latschar's and Henry Funk's homes
instructed the Mennonites that they could not do it.

Yet as more news of possible British attacks circulated,
official letters were sent to the new lieutenants, com-
manding them to get organized as quickly as possible.
The Lititz Moravians told their young men simply to ig-

nore the military enrollment. "It would be better," they
felt, "even if it causes us some suffering," to have nothing
to do with it. In Providence Pastor Muhlenberg began to
receive requests from his Lutheran parishioners for bap-
tismal certificates so that those who were near the
eighteen to fifty-three age limits could prove their ages to
the constables.

The war could be felt approaching. In the *Pennsylvania Evening Post* on April 24 appeared an inflamma-
tory article describing fearful brutalities said to be
perpetrated by the British army, rumored to be receiving
many new German mercenaries. According to the article,
the Redcoats were abusing women with lust and bru-
tality, they had committed savage butchery of people
who had surrendered and been disarmed, they were
guilty of wanton and oppressive devastation of the
country and of inhuman acts in their treatment of
prisoners. It was familiar war rhetoric, to be sure, but not
without its truth. The Hessians, men who had no employment in their own country, were not gentlemanly in their
methods of living off the land.

On the day after this alarming description appeared,
the first class of the militia of five Pennsylvania counties
was called up. All kinds of war preparations now cast a
lurid glow over daily life in Southeastern Pennsylvania.
Three thousand men were under arms in Bucks County,
while in Lancaster County three of the nine battalions
still had not organized. These were the ones, complained
a local official, which were "in the heart of the Mininists
Settlements . . . who pamper with the Constables &
prevent them of making their Returns." Just as irritating
was the way Mennonites refused to sell their produce for

Continental paper money, carrying their "market stuff" from house to house in the town of Lancaster, selling it "very low for hard cash," but carrying it home "sooner than sell it for Congress currency." This happened, it was said, "every market day." Haggling over prices increased, and, in Pastor Muhlenberg's wry opinion, those with "tender consciences" were especially prone to it. And all the while collectors were moving through the townships, requesting blankets, linen, and clothing for the army. Objections to these collections were brushed aside as selfish. No money, but only promise of future payment, was left in the hands of the owners.

Some of the newly appointed militia officers and justices of the peace felt a personal anger toward those who were not enthusiastic for the patriot cause. One such lieutenant was John Wetzel of Macungie Township, not far from the thriving mill of the silenced Preacher Henry Funk, Jr. With Frederick Limbach, a new justice, Wetzel determined to sweep his district free of noncooperators in the war effort. People like him received a handy tool on June 13, 1777, when the Pennsylvania Assembly adopted "an Act obliging the male white inhabitants of this State to give assurance of Allegiance" to their new government. This was to be done before the first day of August, and it was intended to flush out once for all those who, for allegedly "sordid or mercenary reasons" had withheld their service and allegiance from the Commonwealth of Pennsylvania.

It was time to make everyone admit that the Colony was now independent of the king. The terms of the oath were spelled out roundly: the subscriber must swear or affirm, depending on his religious convictions, to "re-

nounce and refuse all allegiance to George the Third,
King of Great Britain," and to "bear true allegiance to the
Commonwealth of Pennsylvania." Not only must he
promise not to do anything "injurious to the freedom and
independence" of the state; he must "make known to
some . . . justice of the peace . . . all treasons and traitorous
conspiracies" against it, of which he might learn. Those
who refused to take the oath would suddenly find
themselves treated as aliens. They could not vote or travel
more than a mile from their homes, nor buy, sell, or
transfer property, nor adopt children. Perhaps worst of
all, there was a provision offering half the fines paid by
violators as a bounty for those who reported them. This
would appeal fully as much to the envy of mean-minded
persons as to their love of American liberty. It brought
memories to the Mennonites of how their ancestors had
lost Swiss farms to jealous neighbors.

This Test Act, which was meant to find out just who
were the Tories with which the area was infested and
make sure that they would not aid an enemy expected to
invade Pennsylvania momentarily, caught the defenseless Christians in a torturous vise. Not even remaining
silently neutral would now be allowed, where the law was
enforced to the letter by choleric officials like John Wetzel
and Frederick Limbach, who now began to harass the
Moravians, Schwenkfelders, and Mennonites in their
neighborhoods. The Moravians of Lititz decided that as
Christians they "could in no wise have anything to do"
with taking back their promise of allegiance to the king.
And even some nonpacifist people around York found
"this long-tailed oath" an unacceptable intrusion on their
freedoms. Persons who would not take it could not have

their word accepted in court, or carry a gun, depending on who was enforcing the law. For some persons, like the Reformed Christian Benner of Franconia Township, it was the means by which their credibility was established at a legal hearing, as when Christian swore that he had been in America for thirty-four years, and was now three years past draft age.

Now and then there was violent reaction to the imposition of these new laws, and one such incident in Lancaster County involved the reputation of the Mennonites. A constable in heavily Presbyterian Donegal Township had heard that a group of "Dutch" people were prepared to "rebel" if he tried to collect from them the fines for declining to exercise with the militia. He wished to collect such a fine from a young man named Samuel Albright, reputed to be a "Menoneast," but he insisted that he would not go without military protection. He had heard that Samuel had "damned" him, and had irreverently demanded, "Who made such laws?"

An officer and six soldiers were sent with the constable, but Samuel Albright had gotten wind of their approach, and had gathered "Twelve men and a number of women, armed with Sithes, Coulters & Pitch forks." The constable tensely informed Samuel that he must now give up either his body or his goods for the fine, and when Samuel would yield neither, asked him to come peaceably along to the magistrate. Sensing the approach of trouble, Samuel's supporters came up close, and Samuel warned the constable's guard that the first man who touched him would be a dead man. Still the soldiers surrounded him. His elderly father Michael tried to cool the dangerous passions, but a deadly battle broke out, and one of

Samuel's defenders caught a Scotch-Irish veteran on the back of the skull with the sharp colter of a plow, splitting it open.

The other soldiers, in fear for their lives, fired the one charge they had in their guns and ran to get more ammunition. Three of the ringleaders had been shot, and Samuel Albright himself lay mortally wounded. Word spread that the three who had been shot were all Mennonites, and that there were perhaps "20 more of the same sect" in a kind of public conspiracy with Quakers to oppose the government. A local official wrote to Philadelphia urging that twelve of the rebels who had been arrested be sent to a Philadelphia jail. There was already a great deal of bad influence, he wrote, by the large number of German mercenary soldiers being kept as prisoners in the area, mostly, it was said, on Mennonite farms.

Whether or not Samuel Albright was a Mennonite, his act was totally alien to the Mennonite teaching. It turned out, in fact, that one of the men arrested as part of the riot on the Albright farm had just returned from a tour of duty with the militia. Yet the word made the rounds that people who pretended nonresistance had killed a man rather than pay a fine of three pounds ten shillings. "A strange picture," observed Pastor Muhlenberg to his diary, "of a tender conscience."

An attitude more typical of the Lancaster Mennonites was displayed by Christian Groff, a young man just beginning to farm in Earl Township. When the sixth class of Captain Crawford's Company was called up for duty, he stayed at home, and was shortly called upon by Lieutenant John Skeible, who requested payment of the usual fine. Christian replied that "he had not the money at the time," but that he was willing to pay if the lieutenant could wait for a few days. The young farmer then sold a horse to raise the money, but by the time the lieutenant came for it, a fire had annihilated all Christian's worldly possessions, including his clothes and the money for his horse. The sympathetic lieutenant then recommended to his superiors that, since such an accident was obviously "vary hard upon a New beginner," his fines for the year 1777 should be written off. Similarly, young John Lapp, of Captain Morgan's company in Hatfield Township in Philadelphia County, was excused of his fines at the end of the year, "He being in very low circumstances and lost a very fine horse which was all his worth."

A related problem was faced by Mennonites who were serving as nonarmed "constables" in areas filled with nonresistant people in Lancaster County. They were asked, along with their nonpacifist colleagues, to prepare lists of the able-bodied men in their communities for militia rosters. When such men as John Newcomer, David Eshelman, Joseph Wenger, and Abraham Witmer refused, they were jailed. Abraham Herr, Witmer's replacement, was indicted for the same offense.

In mid-July of 1777 came the disturbing word that a British army marching down the Hudson River Valley from Canada under General John Burgoyne had chased the Americans headlong from two forts, and had put General Howe, in New York City, in a strong position to invade Pennsylvania and drive on the capital city. In these days of tension men were continuing to take the test oath, after which they were given a small certificate to

carry when traveling. But at least one devout Schwenkfelder, spiritual leader George Kriebel, a neighbor of the
prosperous miller Henry Funk at Hosensack, refused and
paid a considerable price. The trouble began when Squire
Frederick Limbach sent a constable to arrest George's
seventeen-year-old son, Abraham, for neither exercising
with the militia nor paying the fine. George had refused
to pay a fine for his son because the boy had not reached
the minimum draft age of eighteen. George was ordered
to accompany Abraham to a hearing before Squire Limbach, and when they arrived they found Lieutenant
Wetzel also on hand, anxious for a confrontation over the
test oath requirement.

When the squire informed young Abraham that he had
issued a warrant for fines of one pound twelve shillings
sixpence, the bashful country boy, who had never been
before a magistrate, was speechless.

"The meaning," explained the squire, "is this: whether
you be eighteen years old or not."

"No," Abraham found his voice.

"Are you sure of it?"

"Yes."

"Have you any evidence?"

"Yes."

"Who is it?"

"My father."

Limbach then called George over to him and asked,
"How old is your boy?"

"He was seventeen the 26th of last May."

"Can you prove it?"

George said he could give his word for it, or his written
statement. "Well," returned the squire, "your words may

be well enough, but here is an act of the Assembly," which, he went on, meant "that we can't take your Evidence before you take the test prescribed in this Act."

George paused in dismay for a bit, and then said, "I can not take this test at the present time."

Lieutenant Wetzel broke in and asked why not. George replied that there were "a few words in it which keep me back."

"Which words?" Wetzel asked.

The ones, George replied, in which the oath-taker must "renounce and refuse all allegiance to the King, his Heirs, and successors."

"Why can't you give up the allegiance to George the Third?" demanded the lieutenant.

Carefully, George explained his position to his unsympathetic hearers. "I have promised allegiance to him when I was naturalized," he said, "and I am afraid I might be guilty of perjury before God, and in my conscience, and, moreover, it is very uncertain upon which side the victory will fall out. Therefore, I can't do it at the present time."

"So," Wetzel responded, "do you declare yourself for George the Third of Great Britain?"

"No sir," replied the exasperated Schwenkfelder, "I don't declare myself for him." It was simply that he had to wait to see on which side God Almighty would bestow the victory.

"Then you won't take the test?" insisted the lieutenant.

"No sir, not at present, Mr. Wetzel."

"Then I do command the justice that he shall immediately commit you to jail, and I will not depart from

here until I see you secured, and you shall not come clear
from imprisonment at no rate, even if you do pay me a
thousand pounds cash on the nail!"

Aghast, George promised his questioners that he would
be true to the state, as far as lay in his power, in paying
taxes, "carting" or anything they might ask, except for
carrying weapons, which his conscience forbade. But
there was no yielding.

"Well, George," said the squire, "you see I can't help
it. I must send you to jail. You better take the test and stay
at home."

"I can't do it yet," George replied, "but I will consider
the matter and consult my friends about it."

"I will do my utmost," stated Lieutenant Wetzel with
great indignation, "to have all those that will not take this
test drove out of the country."

"But sir," pleaded the Schwenkfelder father, "where
shall they go?"

"They may go to Lord Howe, or wherever they please,
leaving their estates behind, but they shall never come
back again amongst us."

Lord Howe was just then, as a matter of fact, about to
call on Pennsylvania. As George pondered in the Easton
jail this sudden change from the liberties he had
cherished as a naturalized Pennsylvania citizen, the
British general set sail out of New York harbor with 15,
000 troops. On the last day of July his "ships to the
number of 228 sail" were observed off the coast of New
Jersey, and immediately orders were given to Pennsylvania revolutionary officials to collect wagons for the removal of "Stores, Provisions, etc." to places where they
could be guarded in the back country. Unprecedented

excitement gripped the countryside, and President Thomas Warton, Jr., of the Supreme Executive Council informed the militia that since guns were scarce, it was "absolutely necessary that those who have not taken the oath of allegiance be disarmed . . . instantly."

In such a charged atmosphere, it was not long before George Kriebel had as company in the jail his neighbor, miller Henry Funk, Jr., who had also been dealt with by Squire Limbach. Three days earlier the silenced preacher had left his mill to pay a bill he owed for some wheat, and to find whether a local blacksmith had finished a new wagon he had ordered. As his horse trotted by the Buckhorn Tavern on his way home, he heard the voice of a local man, Philip Walter, calling him from a window. Walter came out, as Henry halted, and asked him where he was going. Henry told him.

"Have you a pass?" Walter wanted to know.

Henry replied that he did not. It had not occurred to him that ordinary business travel such as he had done for years would now be suspect.

"You are my prisoner!" snapped Walter, taking the horse's bridle. He then demanded that the tavern-keeper go with him as a witness, as he meant to take the miller to a nearby justice, Squire Frederick Limbach. When the proprietor declined, saying that he was too busy to leave, Walter requested a bystander, Walter Laub, to come along.

"Why are you taking me there?" asked the amazed Henry Funk. "What is the reason?"

"Because you will not take the oath of allegiance," replied the self-appointed constable. "It is our duty to take such people up."

In a short time the party of three stood before Squire Limbach, who wanted to know why Henry could not take the oath.

"It is against my conscience," declared the miller, "because we are supposed to be at peace with everybody and forgive all men." To make a deliberate statement that one would no longer keep an earlier promise of loyalty to a king was not peaceful, let alone honest.

The squire then asked the two accusers whether Henry had actually said anything against the state. When they replied negatively, he gave Henry a day to consider whether he might not, after all, be willing to take the oath.

On the following day the four men met again at Limbach's house, and the squire asked Henry once more what he wished to do regarding the test.

"I have considered the matter well all this time," replied the miller, "and the more I consider it the less liberty I can find in my conscience to take that test."

"If you can't take the oath," was the squire's rejoinder, "I must take the sworn statement of these men."

Henry responded that he himself would give his promise, without an oath, to be true to the state "according to the doctrine of St. Paul [to] be subject to the higher powers." Turning to the two accusers, Mr. Limbach asked if they could swear that they were convinced in their hearts and consciences that Henry was actually a spy. What reason, he asked, did they have for such a suspicion?

"Because he travels forwards and backwards, and refuses to take the oath," was the reply.

The squire then swore the two accusers upon the Bible,

and asked them to state the truth, the whole truth, and nothing but the truth. Then he repeated the question: "What reason have you to suppose that Henry Funk is a spy?"

They repeated the grounds of their suspicions.

"Are you convinced in your conscience that Henry Funk might be a spy?"

"Yes," answered both men.

Henry, who had given his word of allegiance to the British king when he had been naturalized, felt that he simply could not abjure the king now "without wounding his conscience." That would simply be, as his neighbor Christopher Schultz put it, "contradictory to his former oath." And even though Henry's Mennonite brethren had accused him of playing loose with the truth in former civil testimony, he could not bring himself now to go back on his word.

The influential Schwenkfelder Schultz, farmer at nearby Hereford and formerly member of the Berks County Committee of Observation, was a cousin of George Kriebel, and had personal acquaintance with members of the Pennsylvania Assembly. When Henry Funk was sent to the Easton jail to join George Kriebel, Schultz sat down indignantly to write a petition to the Assembly. He accused the militant Squire Limbach of conduct that was a "highly culpable, and daring violation of the . . . Constitution, of the Law, and of his sworn Duty." He requested a hearing on the case, and also wrote a long, passionate protest to a "dear old friend," Sebastian Levan, now serving in the Assembly. He wished to protest the enforcement of laws like the Test Act on the citizens of "once free Pennsylvania," with the resultant fines, imprisonment, and loss of civil rights. "Twenty-five pounds," he wrote sadly, in regard to substitute fines, "are by force and violence taken from one and given to another who will accept eight weeks [military] service. . . . We are freeholders no more; as witnesses we are accepted no more; we are not to step from our own land lest we be driven to Howe or into the wild sea."

And why have their rights been taken away? "Because we are unwilling to take oath concerning things that are of the utmost uncertainty whether we can remain true to the same . . . ." It is preposterous that "in the midst of the hottest warfare and before the conclusion of the matter" we are informed that our "former lord is to be denied under oath." What kind of justice, Christopher asks, sends his cousin George to jail "if he does not swear the way you want him to"? "Have you," he demands, "in your hearts at any time put yourself in the place of these people and viewed . . . their matters of conscience as your own?" Intelligent people "know quite well that Pennsylvania was originally the property of these people who on account of scruples of conscience have misgivings against killing other people and who also consider very carefully before entering, in the place of an oath, upon a course which they cannot be fully assured they can continue in truth. . . ."

The Supreme Council, eager as it was to capture spies, could recognize an overreaction of the kind to which Frederick Limbach was prone. They instructed their secretary to write to the squire and explain the extent of the Test Act carefully, desiring that he would refrain from extending it "beyond what it will fully justify." Henry Funk and George Kriebel were released, and they returned to their Hosensack homes a few days after the troops of George Washington had marched through Philadelphia to head off General Howe, whose fleet was now approaching Pennsylvania through the Chesapeake Bay.

Chapter 8

Washington Visits the Skippack

Preacher Jacob Funk, Jr., son of a first cousin to millers Christian and Henry, had grown up near them on a farm in Indianfield and been ordained as a minister to serve along with Christian. Then at the age of forty-four, five years after Christian had become the local bishop, Jacob had reversed the usual direction of outward migration from the original settlement of Germantown, and bought a farm on the Old York Road about two miles east of the new stone meetinghouse along the peach-tree-lined Germantown Road. Happening within weeks of Paul Revere's visit to Philadelphia asking aid for blockaded Boston, Jacob's removal from Franconia had left a gap among the ministers there, which had been filled by the ordination of Christian Funk's farmer-neighbor Jacob Oberholtzer. The Germantown congregation, small in membership though possessed of a new building, now gained a vigorous and articulate leader.

In the early morning of August 23, 1777, while his cousin Henry was sitting in the Easton jail, Jacob could hear the drums and watch the advancing flags of 8,000 American soldiers marching by his Germantown farm toward Philadelphia. Their destination was Wilmington, a town farther down the Delaware on the other side of Philadelphia, and their assignment was to head off the forces of General Howe which had at last landed in Maryland, and were expected to try to take the rebel capital of Philadelphia. The tramp of the marching columns was muted by the softness of the soldiers' shoes, which they had worn paper thin by their incessant maneuvers in the previous summer.

George Washington, riding with the young French volunteer, The Marquis de Lafayette, had given detailed orders for the conduct of this march. The soldiers' weapons were "well burnished," and each man had stuck a bit of gay greenery in his hat. The "whores and vagabonds" who customarily traveled along with the baggage had been deliberately shunted off to one side of the main route of march, which included Market Street. The idea was to make a favorable impression on the populace of Philadelphia by the strength and spirit of the Continental Army, and to intimidate the many Tories among the citizenry. John Adams, having returned with the rest of the Continental Congress from temporary quarters in Baltimore, and who now realized that they might need to change the location of the government again, thought that the troops lacked the air of distinguished soldiers. "They don't step exactly in time," he wrote his family in Massachusetts. But by nightfall the Army had encamped at Wilmington, where they could wait until the British recouped enough from their storm-wracked voyage to get into motion.

Philadelphia was now a beehive of frantic activity to prepare for a possible invasion. Congress left hastily in the direction of Lancaster, and in the hyper-excitement some forty influential men who were considered dangerous to the cause of liberty were suddenly seized and placed under guard in the Masonic Lodge. David Rittenhouse and three military officers had agreed to help in these arrests, most of which involved Quakers like the merchant Israel Pemberton; his son John, a minister; and Thomas Wharton, Sr., first cousin of the President of the militant Supreme Executive Council, Thomas Wharton, Jr. The "Records & Papers of the Meeting of Sufferings" of the Quakers were also seized, in the suspicion that they might contain information of political significance. Former Governor John Penn and Chief Justice Benjamin Chew, of Germantown near the Mennonite Meetinghouse, were likewise placed under arrest.

These arbitrary and, in the light of history, overly harsh measures were justified on the grounds that they were "necessary for the Public safety of this time when a British Army is landed in Maryland, with a professed design of enslaveing this free Country, & is now advanceing towards this City, as a principal object of hostility." Eventually about half of the arrested men were placed on wagons and shipped to Virginia at their own expense. Two of them died as a result of the hardships involved. Their chagrin and amazement knew no bounds, as they compared their situation with the dream of their founder, William Penn, though their Quaker beliefs limited their defense to written and spoken protests.

Their melancholy wagon train made only a small part of a frenzied exodus that included elegant coaches as well

as farm wagons like that of Mennonite farmer Christian
Weaver of Lancaster County, borrowed for the occasion.
Every spare vehicle that could be located was pressed into
service of Philadelphians who wished to get out before a
battle or invasion occurred. A proclamation by the
Supreme Executive Council assured them that Howe's
armies were bent on plunder and devastation, and that
they faced "an enemy than whom none more cruel and
perfidious was ever suffered to vex and destroy any
people." Philadelphians were asked to "Seriously
consider . . . the wanton ravages, the Rapes, the But-
cheries which have been perpetrated by these men in the
State of New Jersey . . . ; above all consider the mournful
prospect of seeing Americans like the wretched inhabitants of India, stripped of their freedom, robbed of
their property, degraded beneath the brutes, & left to
starve amid plenty, at the will of their lordly Masters, and
let us determine once or for all, that we will *Die or be
Free.*" The proclamation closed with the expression of
the hope that "by the goodness of the Almighty, the Lord
of Hosts & God of Battles," the British army would be
"wholly delivered into our hands." Immediately under
the signatures of the president and the secretary appeared
the words, "GOD SAVE THE PEOPLE."

As the Quaker exiles were being carted out of the city,
the distant boom of cannon could be heard from a
southeasterly direction. It was the first major clash of the
war to take place on Pennsylvania soil. Washington with
11,000 men had tried to block the advance of the Redcoats at the Brandywine Creek in Chester County, but
was being outmaneuvered and, suffering 1,000 casualties,
forced to retreat toward Chester. Seventeen-year-old Ab-

raham Funk, apparently a nephew of Bishop Christian, was one of the innumerable "carters." It would be related in years to come that, during the retreat, he had run down to the creek with buckets that were carried on the side of his family's wagon, and had scooped up water for his horses, which he held to their thirsty mouths so they could drink as they pulled along without stopping. The battle raged close to a rural Quaker meetinghouse, where a monthly meeting was being held on the fringes of the hellish slaughter. Inside it was "quiet and peaceful," as one of the participants remembered, notwithstanding the fact that, in the words of another, it "was a very trying time. The British army was marching through the neighborhood, and . . . it was difficult for Friends to get there."

Wagonloads of wounded men rattled off toward Bethlehem, Ephrata, and Lititz, the victims crying out in anguish when the wheels thudded over a rock or a hole. Washington ordered the Army's supplies carted toward Bethlehem, and a train of 700 wagons accompanied by 200 soldiers arrived on the evening of September 24. "In one night," wrote a local observer, the soldiers "destroyed all our buckwheat and the fences around the fields." In the meantime Washington's Army had marched west on the Lancaster Road, and had just opened fire on the British when a torrential rain wet down their powder so thoroughly that both sides had to quit. Determined to get pouches with flaps that would keep out rainwater, Washington headed north to guard his supplies, after destroying a forge along the Schuylkill in a Quaker community.

He marched his troops east across the Schuylkill River, chest high, at Parker's Ford, not far from the homes of

Mennonite farmer Jacob Longacre and Brethren Pastor Martin Urner. As the hungry men passed through the well-tended countryside Washington observed "with the utmost concern the continual Straggling of Soldiers on the March, who rob Orchards & commit other disorders & that many Officers pay little or no Attention to prevent" this "mischievous" practice. Although the generals of both sides issued many orders against pillage by their own men, they could exercise only partial control. For every order not to steal food they had to issue another for soldiers to take produce or horses or hay or wagons in the name of their authority. By the time either army had passed by a farm, anything visible that was edible by man or beast had been taken.

The British Army now appeared to be pursuing the Yankees north along the west side of the Schuylkill. On the evening of September 21 horsemen galloped excitedly past the mill of Mathias Pennypacker, later to serve as a Mennonite bishop, and announced that the Redcoats were coming. When the soldiers did indeed arrive that evening, the Third Brigade camped on Mathias' farm, while the Hessian general Knyphausen had his headquarters at the house of Mathias' neighbor Frederick Bosshart. Miller Pennypacker had moved to the banks of Pickering Creek from his native Skippack only a few years before, and built a fine new mill close to the main road leading north from Valley Forge. No more than his Quaker or Episcopalian neighbors had he foreseen a civil war approaching. But now their lives were disrupted in the pattern reminiscent of European political troubles. A man named Yost, working for Mathias in his mill, was called for by militia officers, and commanded to come away at once for service in his designated company. He was asked to leave before he would be able to change his dusty clothes. When Mr. Yost refused to leave his work, he was seized against his will, and rushed off to the militia bareheaded.

But now it was the British who confiscated all Mathias Pennypacker's grain and flour, broke up the mill-machinery, and cut the bolting cloth to shreds to prevent its being used by the Americans. This may have been in retaliation for the destruction of Valley Forge by the Americans. Such malice was in the starkest contrast to the conscientious manners of the miller, who would not permit locks or keys to be used in his house, and who, when lending money, would take no bond or note.

The bitter fruits of war were now reaped by the local populace in good earnest. Three daughters of one of Pennypacker's farmer neighbors were dragged to the British camp for the soldiers' sexual enjoyment, and where the American Army lay, on the other side of the Schuylkill, women and girls bent pillows over their heads and ears to block out the blood-curdling screams of soldiers whose wounded limbs had become gangrenous, and now had to be amputated.

To Washington's dismay, it soon became evident that the British pursuit had been a trick. The Redcoats suddenly turned back and, on a pleasant Tuesday, waded across the Schuylkill to Norriton Township, where they now were encamped strategically between the Americans and Philadelphia. Having again been outmaneuvered, Washington complained that he had been able to gather no trustworthy information about British movements, since everybody in the countryside through which he had marched was out of sympathy with the American cause. The British view of the situation was precisely opposite— that the people were "very rebellious." They observed Benjamin Rittenhouse's manufacturing of "Shot and Cannon," and, in their foraging during a temporary halt gave a bad scare to the children of Benjamin's brother Henry. Six of them ran onto the woods as British soldiers approached their home, while Mrs. Rittenhouse hid a visiting young woman in a closet, and shoved a cupboard in front of it. The soldiers, though they gathered some food and clothing, were dissatisfied with their loot, and split open the door of the cupboard without noticing the closet behind it.

The military excitement caused the Schwenkfelders to disperse early, on Wednesday, September 24, from a meeting at Hosensack, near the mill of Henry Funk. It was the annual apple-butter meal, a thanksgiving for their safe arrival from Europe in Pennsylvania forty-three years earlier. A rumor had arrived that the British were marching in their direction, and families quickly dispersed to their unguarded homes.

The British, as it became clear two days later, were headed in the opposite direction—toward Philadelphia. At half-past eight on a rough, windy morning they rode south from Norriton, and an hour and a half later entered the city with a band solemnly playing "God Save the King." The main body of the Redcoats, including the Hessians, were left behind in Chestnut Hill and Germantown, where they rapidly used up and took all of Preacher Jacob Funk's possessions, until nothing was left of his farm but the land and the buildings.

A disappointed Washington immediately gave orders

for his troops to draw closer to the city, and by four o'clock that afternoon had, with beating drums, moved 8,000 Continentals and 2,000 militia to an encampment along the Perkiomen Creek near the original Mennonite settlement of Skippack, next in age to the Germantown community. By nightfall the Army had carried away for campfires every fence on the farm of Mennonite miller Samuel Pennypacker. Four stacks of unthreshed wheat disappeared, with all the hay and straw in the barn. Every chicken that could be found was eaten. Washington noted with irritation, during his stay at Pennypacker's Mills, that "the base and wicked practice of plundering the Inhabitants is still continued, notwithstanding all orders, & in some cases in the most atrocious manner."

Miller Pennypacker, a close relative of Mathias Penny-packer whose mill-machinery had been ruined by the British several days earlier, was left stripped of all his crops. As he gazed over the restless army, it appeared to him three times as large as it actually numbered. After it left he was to write in the margin of his large family Bible, "On the 26th of September, 1777, an army of 30,000 men encamped in Skippack Township, burned all the fences, carried away all the fodder, hay, oats, and wheat and took their departure. . . . Written for those who come after me. Samuel Pennypacker." A neighbor of Samuel's, a Men-nonite bachelor named John Weirman, received a call from an American officer who wished to buy grain. John stated that he did not wish to sell any, whereupon the of-ficer raised his gun and sent a ball through the front door of John's farmhouse, on through another door between two rooms, and into the opposite wall. John, at this point, became willing to sell grain to the American Army.

As for Pastor Muhlenberg of nearby Providence, on the day after the new encampment had taken place, he received one of the shocks of his life. He had come to his Lutheran church at "The Trappe" to bury the child of one of his deacons, when he was horrified to see the building crowded with militiamen carrying guns. Up in the organ loft one of the soldiers was playing an accompaniment to his companions' rowdy songs. The floor was spread with straw and manure, and on the altar were the remnants of a meal. Entering the church cautiously, the outraged minister kept still, but a soldier yelled up to the organist, "Play a Hessian march!"—an obvious taunt as to the pastor's German background. Muhlenberg found a colonel and asked him if this was what the Americans meant by "religious and civil liberty." The officer apologized by saying that it was impossible to impose discipline on such a miscellany of nationalities. The pastor was also depressed to find his three-acre field of buckwheat, just then "in fine bloom," trampled down by twenty horses and cattle which had been turned into the plot by the soldiers. "If one objects with the merest word," Muhlenberg wrote in his diary, "one is told 'You are a *Tory*! Your house and home must be burned!' " At the same time, he noted, "Those on the other side say, 'You are rebels.' "

Five miles away at Pennypacker's Mills the pastor's son, General Peter Muhlenberg, wrote in his own order book on the same day the instructions he had received from Washington: "As the Troops will rest today, Divine service is to be performed in all the Corps which have Chaplains. . . ." This was a Saturday, and the ceremonials of the following Sunday were not precisely religious.

Amazingly good news had arrived, of a hardly expected
and overwhelming victory of the Northern American
Army over the British General Burgoyne in New York.
Washington gave orders that his troops at Pennypacker's
Mills be "paraded and served with a Gill of Rum" each, at
four in the afternoon, and that thirteen cannon—one for
each colony—be fired. As the heavy booming rang out
over the Sabbath stillnes, everyone from Christian Funk
on the Indian Creek to Pastor Muhlenberg in the opposite
direction could hear the thundering echoes. Muhlenberg
counted fourteen shots, and noticed the militia encampment around his church sounding an alarm on their
drums, apparently in the mistaken notion "that there
might be a battle on the Skippack."

Washington, in conference at Pennypacker's Mills with
sixteen generals, now planned to test General Howe's
mettle in Philadelphia. Among those who dissented, feeling that an attack on an entrenched enemy was too dangerous, was General Francis Nash of North Carolina. But
his commander ruled that his Army would move closer
and aggressively probe for "a proper opening." On the
morning after the celebration the Army marched off from
Pennypacker's Mills, leaving the area looking as if a
swarm of locusts had been here. One Schwenkfelder
farmer turned in a bill for 3,228 fence rails as they left.

At six o'clock on Saturday night, October 3, the men
were under arms, and began a secret night march toward
Germantown, now guarded by the bulk of Howe's Army.
The British commander himself was five miles farther
down, in Philadelphia. The American generals were
instructed to bring their troops down four separate roads
converging on Germantown. The underfed, poorly

clothed, and often barefoot troops were maneuvered into
position before sunrise, except for those under the direction of General Smallwood, who were to have approached
by way of the Old York Road past the farm of Jacob Funk,
but had lost their way in the darkness. Precisely at five in
the morning the Americans rushed in on the British, who
quickly took up positions in the substantial stone houses
lining the main street of the two-mile-long, narrow
village. Just as the sun was rising, a dense fog settled in,
which, with the billowing gunsmoke, made it impossible
to see for any distance.

As the Americans pushed rapidly down the main road,
a group of British soldiers found themselves cut off from
their companions. They rushed into the nearby stone
mansion of former Chief Justice Benjamin Chew, who
had been sent to Virginia as a Tory detainee. Their
presence in this house behind the American lines worried
General Henry Knox into persuading Washington that
they must be removed before the Americans could safely
advance further. Somewhat reluctantly, Washington
ordered up reserve troops to take the mansion, but a
lieutenant walking up to the building carrying a flag of
truce to demand surrender was shot down. Then three-
pound cannon balls were bounced off the thick walls,
with no effect. Soldiers who tried to storm the windows
were bayoneted. Volunteers attempting to fire the building were also killed. The American thrust had stalled.

For two and a half hours Germantown rocked with
gunfire and the hoarse screams of command and death, as
every hedge and garden was bitterly contested. Jacob
Funk's twelve-year-old daughter Elizabeth, who happened to be in a home near the action, hid in a cellar. Just

beyond the Mennonite meetinghouse was the home of
Jacob Keyser, who, with John Keyser, helped with the
wounded. At one point the American soldiers fired mistakenly at each other, and in a confused panic began to
retreat. General Francis Nash, at this juncture, received a
massive wound in his thigh from a cannon ball which
killed his horse, and had to be carried out of the fray.

The British General Howe, who for a while had
thought he was staring into the face of defeat, now rallied
his men with the arrival of his colleague General
Cornwallis, who had double-timed up from Philadelphia
with reinforcements. As they advanced out the main road
past the Mennonite meetinghouse, British General James
Agnew rode at the head of his Fourth Brigade, but suddenly toppled from his horse when a shot ran out from a
sniper behind the wall of the graveyard. Elizabeth Engel,
a member of the congregation, watched as several men
carried the mortally wounded general past her door. The
identity of the sniper would never be publicly revealed,
though a local half-wit would in later years claim the
credit.

Finally the Americans, who had earlier been cheering
in Market Square over what they had thought was victory, were in full and panic-filled retreat, having lost 152
killed, 521 wounded, and about 400 captured. The admitted British toll was about half that figure. Gradually fear
worsened in the American ranks, as the British pursued
them over roads red with "a great amount of blood" to a
considerable distance north of Germantown. Many of the
fleeing troops, though they had had no food for twenty-
four hours, could not bring themselves to rest until they
had fled all the way back to Pennypacker's Mills. As they

struggled, bone-weary, over the Skippack Creek, they were observed by Mennonite children who walked out their narrow farm lanes to the Skippack Road. Long after the war it would be remembered how the mother of one of the Dutch-speaking Jansen families had carried soup and other food out to the road for the famished men. Some said that sick soldiers had actually been taken in to the Jansen farm until they recuperated.

Back in Germantown several of Jacob Keyser's boys peered in fascination at the dead bodies of soldiers sprawled in their streets and gardens. Thinking it would hurt no one, they removed several buckles from the shoes of the fallen men, but when they took them home father Keyser made it firmly clear that there would be no stealing even from the dead, and the boys took the buckles out to bury them with their former owners.

Wagonloads of wounded men stopped overnight outside a tavern in Franconia Township at the edge of Deacon Christian Meyer's farm. The night-long groans wrenched the hearts of neighbors, who found dogs licking up puddles of blood after the wagons had moved on. A soldier who died en route was buried in a graveyard on George Delp's farm, near the grave of Bishop Henry Funk. Crowds of soldiers swarmed over the farm of Abraham Allebach in nearby Hatfield Township, and the Mennonite school and meetinghouse near Pennypacker's Mills served as one of the many hospitals. A huge circular grave was dug nearby for those dying of their wounds. Many sick and wounded men were simply quartered in local farmhouses, as was General Nash, who, though he had gallantly borne his pain as he was carried out to Towamencin on a litter of poles, was now bleeding through two featherbeds. The houses of the Moravian communities at Bethlehem and Lititz, the Ephrata Cloister, and the churches of other denominations were jammed with sick and wounded men.

Washington, now back at "Camp near Pennypacker's Mill," was severely disappointed by the apparent victory turned into defeat, but thought it proved at least that the Americans could seriously challenge the British forces, and would impress potential American allies such as France. Mindful of approaching winter, the general immediately ordered the further collection of "blankets, shoes, stockings, and other articles of clothing," to be taken from various parts of the countryside, "giving receipts therefor." It is especially "recommended," he wrote, to obtain "these things from the Quakers and dissatisfied inhabitants," but the point, "at all events," is "to get them."

On the third day after the battle a delegation of Philadelphia Quakers arrived, as a matter of fact, to confer with Washington in his camp along the Perkiomen. The six men had already been to see Lord Howe in Philadelphia, and they now wished to present to the commander of the other side the testimony of their people against war, and plead for their brethren who had been shipped to Virginia. Waiting their turn among the generals counseling with Washington, they distributed printed statements of their position, declaring that they were not on either side of the present polarization. Washington received them kindly and gave them their dinner before directing them to stay north of the camp for a few days so that they could not possibly carry intelligence back into the city immediately.

Though Washington's main intention was to rest and refresh the men, and to recover the Army from "that disorder naturally attendant on a retreat," he decided, in a few days, to move them once again closer to Philadelphia. Concerned with such matters as proper greasing of cartridge pouches, shoes for his barefoot men, the lack of sufficient officers, General Nash's worsening condition, and the exemplary punishment of a soldier who had attempted to desert to the British, he gave orders for the Army to encamp along the Skippack Creek in Towamencin Township, near what he called a "Baptist meetinghouse." This was the homestead of the pioneer Bishop Jacob Gaedtschalck, and a part of the charge, since his death, of the present Bishop Andrew Ziegler. It was the home of the Towamencin Mennonite congregation, located along the Maxatawny Road a mile east of its ford of the Skippack.

Here, among the meadows and fields of Schwenkfelder, Mennonite, Reformed, and Lutheran farm families, the Army encamped for nine days, while its general pondered another attack on Philadelphia. The 8,000 men began to dwindle, as militiamen left for home, their tours of duty expiring, and others deserted. Gradually new troops arrived. General Pulaski, white-clad Polish leader of Washington's cavalry, stayed in a farmhouse of the Schwenkfelder Minister Christopher Hoffman, while Washington was quartered nearby at Frederick Wambold's. The soldiers hacked down the forests on both sides of the Skippack for their campfires to ward off the October chill, and carried off Henry Cassel's fence in spite of strict orders to the contrary. Every now and then a rumor that the British were coming would

sweep through the camp with such conviction that a
number of doctors fled with their patients, who were carried on litters, to the more remote regions of Oley to the
northwest.

During the encampment the Congress, now meeting in
the town of York, passed a resolution forbidding the carrying of provisions to Philadelphia. This activity had
been, for many Mennonites, an important means of income. The British, who now controlled the city, paid in
gold and silver for the produce they bought, while the
American Army continued to use the cheap paper
"Continentals." This particular issue would grow in importance over the next half year until it became deadly
serious.

One bit of business that had been left over from the
previous encampment was the execution of the deserter
John Farndon. This had been scheduled for Thursday,
October 9, but was once again postponed when it became
necessary to have a funeral for General Nash and several
other officers who had become casualties of the Germantown slaughter. The nearest graveyard was that of
the Mennonite Meeting at Towamencin, and thus it happened that on a cold, rainy morning of October, 1777, a
general was buried with full military honors in the God's
Acre of the defenseless Christians. Washington stood by
with his generals and the Army drawn up in parade, as an
oration was given and cannon bellowed over the four
caskets. Once again the people for many miles around,
hearing what Pastor Muhlenberg thought was "sharp
cannonading," were alarmed by fears of approaching
war.

The following day was remembered all their lives by a

large group of local boys who had gathered to watch the
hanging of the deserter. Detachments of sixty soldiers
from each of twelve brigades had been ordered to parade
at the hanging. As the doomed prisoner was brought
beneath a large tree near the Skippack, young John
Boorse, from a nearby Mennonite farm, and his companions saw General Washington suddenly mount a horse
and order a group of soldiers to form a ring around the
man about to be hanged, in order, the disappointed boys
gathered, to close off their view of the morbid scene.

It was during the Towamencin encampment, in which
the visiting Dr. Benjamin Rush could see nothing but
"bad bread; no order; universal disgust," that General
Washington again received the most heartening news
imaginable. General Burgoyne had again been decisively
defeated by the Northern American Army. If indeed the
menace to the north were now to be eliminated, the
Americans could concentrate their energies on expelling
General Howe from Philadelphia. Once again "thirteen
pieces of Cannon" were discharged "in Honour of the
Northern Army." Such a victory made ridiculous the letter handed to Washington on the very same day, written
by an Episcopalian rector in Philadelphia, calling on the
general to halt his campaign, since his cause was regarded
as militarily hopeless. Washington severely reprimanded
the woman who had risked her life to bring the letter to
his headquarters by the Skippack.

Though for politicians and generals war is diagramed
along abstract lines far over the heads of the common
people, these latter folk who must shoot the guns, be shot,
and pay the costs of the politicians' and generals' decisions, understand war too. They remember it differently

than do the excellent gentlemen in the legislatures and
command headquarters. The cattle they have bred and
fed, the silverware in their kitchens, the clothing they
have woven and sewn are given up with reluctance. At
Towamencin one man hid in a pile of sheep manure to escape the notice of the soldiers, and another, who objected
to the ransacking of his house, was put in a pen on his own
farm to keep him from obstructing the cause of liberty.
The soldiers themselves were endlessly famished. One
poor young private who fell upon a honeycomb in the
woods along the Skippack partook all too immoderately,
and soon lay, beyond all appetite, among the peaceful
Schwenkfelder graves beneath unspoiled oaks that were
somehow spared the axes of the encampment.

The farmer and his family go on with their quiet lives
while the politicians and generals direct their tumultuous
movements. By Indian Creek, in the lap of the next valley
to the Skippack, deacon Henry Rosenberger's family is
celebrating the wedding of his daughter Magdalena to his
indentured servant, John Swartley. John has had to pay
considerable fines to stay clear of the militia. This is his
happy day; the harvest is in, it is wedding season, and the
sumptuous meal is nearly prepared. But there are unex-
pected guests. The inevitable foragers have come across
the rise from Towamencin, seeking supplies for the Army.
The women consult in consternation; they agree on a
plan; they invite the soldiers to sit down with the guests.
There is friendship and respect in the midst of the chaos
of war, and the soldiers, having drunk to the health of the
newlyweds, leave without taking so much as a chicken.
The events of this strange wedding day will be remembered and told by several grandmothers who have

never heard the patriot name of General Francis Nash, whose torn body now rests in the graveyard side by side with those of their defenseless relatives of Towamencin, and whose memory will one day be honored by a yet unborn city in Tennessee.

Chapter 9

That Memorable Winter

The month and a half between Washington's breaking
camp at Towamencin and his establishing winter quarters
across the Schuylkill was a time of tentativeness and tension. Christopher Saur, the Germantown printer, whose
son was becoming something of a spy for the British, and
who had observed the forcible removal of the Quaker pacifists, became increasingly nervous with the hovering
approach of the Rebel Army, and moved to British-con-
trolled Philadelphia. Daily Washington's generals considered attacking the capital, only a two hours' march
from their camp, and they edged still closer, picking high
sites like Worcester Hill.

Feeling the pinch of desertion and the expiration of
tours of duty among the militia, Washington was
disgusted with the little interest taken in the war by local
well-to-do people. "I assure you, sir," he wrote to the
president of Pennsylvania's Council, "it is a matter of astonishment to every part of the Continent to hear that
Pennsylvania, the most opulent and populous of all the

states, has but twelve hundred militia in the field." The same lack of enthusiasm was evident in regard to supplying Pennsylvania's quota for the regular Army. "Your battalions," Washington complained, "have never been one third full, and now many of them are far below even that."

The Council of Safety could not deny these embarrassing facts, and acknowledged, a week after receiving Washington's letter, "the delinquency of the Personal service of many Male inhabitants in this State," along with their failure to pay fines which could be used to hire substitutes. If the citizens were so lacking in desire to be delivered from threatened "slavery," they must be forced by law to cooperate. Once again an "Ordinance" was passed, "for the more effectual levying" of substantial fees, and even the retroactive collection of the "many . . . fines . . . for nonattendance" of the militia-exercises which had been held under the now defunct Association.

A considerable number of men who were out of sympathy with the war had simply ignored the fines thus far. In York County, where the Congress was now sitting, there were "so many scrupolis people," according to a local lieutenant, that the militia companies were "hard to be filled up." In the neighborhoods made up of "mostly Irish People" there was no such difficulty. But the "Grate Number of Quakers, Mananest & Dunkers" in other areas were said to "deter the business much." A similar situation in Lancaster County was met by the appointment of extra Sublieutenants to collect fines, which were now backed by jail sentences.

Washington's discouragement over Pennsylvania's lack of support was relieved by the nearly unbelievable good news, received at Worcester on October 18, that General Burgoyne had actually surrendered with the whole northern British Army. This threw a whole new light on the military situation, and would make much more likely the respect of European countries for the Revolutionary regime. It would relieve the growing pressure on Washington by even some of his own officers, who had begun to wonder if the faltering American cause needed a better general.

"Let every face brighten," Washington now exhorted his troops, "and every heart expand with grateful joy and praise to the Supreme Disposer of all events, who has granted us this success." Chaplains were ordered to "prepare short discourses" for the occasion of rejoicing at Camp Worcester, and immediately after these had been delivered, thirteen cannon were once more fired, followed by a *feu de joie*—in which every soldier fired a blank cartridge from his rifle—and "three huzzas." The shock of the cannon blast was so great, it would later be claimed, that most of the windows in the home of Peter Wentz, Washington's headquarters, were shattered.

All this was doubtless less important to the Mennonite farmer Henry Cassell than the 696 fence rails the soldiers had burned, and for which he now submitted a bill of eight pounds fourteen shillings, witnessed by Frederick Wambold, Washington's host at the Towamencin encampment.

It had been in Wambold's house, on a rise above the Skippack Creek, that the brilliant Philadelphia physician Benjamin Rush had reached a peak of disgust. He had thought it unseemly for Washington to sit two or three places from the head of the table, and for the cooks to have only half enough knives and forks, so that the company had to eat in two shifts. The lack of discipline, ragged troops, indiscriminate firing of guns—it all seemed part of a half-baked campaign. But then Dr. Rush always had strong opinions, such as his low regard for the culture of the Pennsylvania German farmers, while at the same time he admitted their earthy practicality. When he arrived at Bethlehem a few weeks after the Skippack movement encampment, and found the Moravian buildings packed so full of sick and wounded soldiers that the surgeons were refusing to admit any more, Dr. Rush suggested that seventy patients be removed to a nearby farm of the Geissingers, a Mennonite family some of whom would shortly suffer the worst effects of the Test Act.

For Washington, now a few miles from Worcester at Whitemarsh, the present task was to find some means of clothing and feeding his shrinking army, while preventing the British from consuming American supplies. His order for soldiers to remove the millstones from mills near Philadelphia brought an indignant letter from General Howe, but Washington in turn reminded Howe of what the Redcoats had done for millers like Matthias Pennypacker. Regarding his own men, it was with "real grief" that Washington observed their barefoot, blanketless misery. While agents were sent out to collect without delay blankets, shoes, stockings, and cloth from people who had not taken the oath of allegiance, the General observed that this "seizing & forcing supplies from the inhabitants" tended to embitter the people without procuring many supplies. He recommended that the state legislatures "resolve on an immediate assessment" on the citizens, in addition to the other taxes, rather than depending upon "seizing by the army." In Lancaster County "about one hundred Waggons" were demanded, just at this time, for the purpose of "supplying the Army with Provisions." Two weeks later Christian Bowman, Peter Witmer, Christian Hershey, and Benjamin Miller were called before the authorities to answer a complaint that they had "not performed their Agreement" in regard to their "Waggons."

While Washington tried vainly to stop farmers from continuing their usual market trips to Philadelphia, his own men grew ever hungrier. Stripping the countryside bare of trees and provender, they left little behind that was edible. When the British swept out toward White-marsh to test Washington's strength, Hessian soldiers "committed great outrages" among homes the Americans had spared. One Rockhill family later told how they had saved their smoked meat by burying it. A poor, famished private from the state of Maine picked through the leavings of a cattle-slaughter site in the Whitemarsh camp, finding, to his delight, an ox pancreas "which had escaped the hogs and dogs." His hunger was such that he took it to his tent, broiled it and gulped it down, only to have it spew out again faster than it had gone in.

But the trials of the late fall were bearable compared to the outright starvation and freezing that faced Washington's army when they finally crossed the Schuylkill and began to build huts on the slopes of Valley Forge. The General immediately sent out an announcement to all persons residing within seventy miles of his head-quarters to see that at least half of their grain crop was threshed out in the next two months. Whatever was left in sheaves after March 1 might be seized by the Army and paid for at the going rate for straw.

Gradually all the trees around the camp began to disappear, as cold settled in with a three-day snow beginning on Christmas Day. Foraging parties roamed the countryside, with the British likewise sallying boldly out from Philadelphia among rich German and Quaker farms. The wife of Amishman Christian Zook, who lived several miles west of Valley Forge, was visited by American soldiers just as she took her family's bread out of the oven, all of which they confiscated except one loaf which she was said to have wrapped in her apron, crying, "This one is for me!"

In Philadelphia there was enough to eat, though prices were high. The British had hard money for the purchase of supplies. General Howe issued a call for "all Intrepid Able-bodied Heroes" who were willing to serve King George against "a tyrannical Congress" while the "present Rebellion" should last. The reward would be "50 acres of Land, where every gallant Hero may retire, and enjoy his Bottle and Lass." Lord Howe was widely known to have his own favorite lass in bed already, and his luxurious, leisurely living scandalized the neutral Quakers. Nevertheless a considerable number of American soldiers deserted to his forces during this cruel winter.

To Christopher Saur, having now fled to the British-held capital, the outlook for 1778 was bleaker than ever before in America. The almanacs he published for this year depicted his "once so happy land" of Pennsylvania as "Oppressed by rapine, murder and a thousand foes." And out in Lancaster, whither David Rittenhouse had fled on the approach of the British, the astronomer considered the sad possibility that "Providence" had "espoused the cause of our enemies," though he could not understand the reasons. He hesitated to visit his wife on the Rittenhouse farm in Norriton for "more than one night," for fear of the British "parties of horse" which might sweep up from Philadelphia and catch him there with her. In another room of the house occupied by Rittenhouse, Tom Paine snored by the hour in an easy chair. Now and then he went for a walk, or wrote two or three sentences in his fifth installment of "Common Sense."

To have his men starve amid plenty was a fate Washington could not accept. He gave strict orders for guards to be placed on each of the nine "Capital roads" that led north from Philadelphia between the Schuylkill and Delaware Rivers. John Lacey, who had been raised as a Bucks County Quaker, was commissioned a Brigadier General in the Pennsylvania militia, with the assignment of keeping small parties of the British from leaving the city, and cutting off the traditional marketing. This proved extremely difficult, for a number of reasons. The 1,000 members of the militia companies involved dwindled, by mid-February, to the point that many roads were said to have no guards within twenty miles of the city. People from Germantown, Washington was informed, were known to "carry immense supplies to the Philadelphia markets," even though he had tried to cut off Germantown from the country above it. The guards responsible to stop this traffic were so "corruptible" that someone suggested employing Indians for the task.

Just as serious as the problem of food reaching the British was the movement of spies. One American officer, in fact, went to the Philadelphia market disguised as a

Quaker farmer, until he realized that he was recognized. Continental money was extremely weak for twenty miles around the city, as "the hope of getting to market" induced many farmers to deny to the foragers of the American Army that they had produce for sale. The simplest supplies, such as fodder for the cattle, were exhausted, and many horses died.

Already in January the bakehouse at the Valley Forge was the scene of court-martials for civilians who persisted in going to market in Philadelphia. The whipping post was a favorite punishment. For sneaking cattle into Philadelphia one man received "250 lashes on his back, well laid on," and another had all his property confiscated, while he went to jail. "Carrying flour" to the city earned Philip Culp fifty lashes and employment "in publick work while the British Army continues in this State." Before long the whippings became so common and so fierce that a surgeon was appointed to stand by, "who stopped several whippings because the culprit could stand no more." One Mennonite farmer who, according to a story told by his family in later years, did get into Philadelphia with his produce, was considered a possible spy by the British, and locked up. All during the night, went the story, Abraham Hunsberger sang hymns undauntedly, and in the morning his captors released him as harmless. Two young men from the community of Christian Funk, Isaac Benner and John Souder, were also observed carrying provisions to the city.

"No meat! No meat!" rose the melancholy chant among the gaunt soldiers shivering beside the fires that had now denuded Valley Forge of its woods. Daily, the near-starving men roamed the nearby countryside, look-

ing for food and something to wear. Nearby, miller
Mathias Pennypacker hid some of his neighbors' clothing
in barrels at the mill. The irascible General Wayne became so annoyed with the complaints of a farmer living
four miles from the camp, whose property had been
repeatedly raided by foragers, that he snapped back one
morning, "Well, damn 'em, shoot 'em—why in the Devil
don't you shoot 'em?" This intemperate advice was taken
all too seriously by the angry farmer, when, a few days
later, he saw yet another soldier in his barnyard, busily
milking one of the cows. The farmer strode into the
house, came out with a gun, and summarily dispatched
the hungry intruder. When arrested and tried by court-
martial, the farmer escaped with his life only by proving
that the fiery General Wayne had indeed made his un-
fortunate suggestion.

Just when the men were most famished, an aggravating
loss of a drove of 130 "very fine" fat cattle was reported.
They had been driven down from New York, had crossed
the Delaware, and reached the Bethlehem Road when
some British soldiers, tipped off by Tories from Hatfield Township, seized them and steered them into
Philadelphia. Deeply irritated, Washington sent out an
appeal for the farmers of the Middle States to fatten immediately as many of their cattle as they could spare.
Later in the year, he promised, they would be paid "a
bountiful price" for their stock by the Army. Other orders
had called for the removal of all "horses, cattle, sheep &
provender" in the region so that the British would not
find them. The Americans learned that the British were
"preparing for a grand forage . . . probably in Bucks
County." To their chagrin, as one of their officers wrote,

they had "the same business in contemplation in the same place."

Having been seriously criticized for letting the British make off with the drove of cattle, General John Lacey instructed one of his scouting parties, in mid-March, that if they met any more people going to market they should "fire upon the villains," leaving them on the road, "their bodies and the marketing lying together." The requirements of military logic had now dramatically superseded the peaceful teaching under which the general had grown up in his Bucks County Quaker boyhood. A week after he issued this drastic order a Mennonite farmer from nearby Bedminster Township turned up among the prisoners. At his court-martial he was convicted of carrying butter and eggs to Philadelphia. The local colonel devised a special punishment for Matthias Tyson. His gray horse having been confiscated, he was stripped to his waist and tied to a large tree. A dozen soldiers, it was said, were then placed ten paces away, and at the order, "Fire!" they splattered his cringing body with the eggs he had been carrying to market. When he was released, it was with the warning that the next time he was caught traveling toward the city he would be unceremoniously shot. But a week or two later General Lacey received instructions from Washington to refrain from any executions, and even "corporal punishment . . . especially if they are people who have any reputable friends in the country."

How, some historians hymning the Revolution have wondered, could these tender-conscienced Christians have been so hardhearted as to let the Continental soldiers starve while they went blandly on with their customary marketing? At the very least, was it not sheer hypocrisy to keep one's goods when offered paper money, and sell them for gold?

Their behavior certainly had a strong economic element. "Since we do not know yet which side will gain the victory," mused Lutheran Pastor Muhlenberg, "the people are fearful." If the Rebels win, Continental money will perhaps retain its value, but in the event of a British victory it will be worthless. No one, obviously, would gladly chance losing the fruits of his labor unless it was in a cause worthy of the risk. But here was a cause with which the defenseless Christians disagreed, and with them, a significant part of Pennsylvania's nonpacifist populace. Moralistic condemnation of their material instincts will carry little weight if it entirely overlooks the fact that these people were trying to ignore a war forced on them by neighbors who identified their own political views with the divine truth, and based this on what they could require at the point of a bayonet. This was an old story to the Mennonites, who had the manuscript poems of Yelles Cassel with them, bemoaning the disruption of their quiet farm life in the Palatinate, as the worldly powers about them used their fields and barnyards as the arena for their struggles. There are some laws, as Abraham Lincoln would later write, that are not laws, but violence. They are "conceived in violence . . . maintained in violence, and . . . executed in violence." Invoking the name of God, and the atmosphere of morality, for what is demanded at the mouth of a cannon has its own hypocrisies.

Looking beyond the squabbles of governments and the vitriol of men who claimed that there could be no resolution but by powder and shot, the defenseless farmers saw that the suffering soldiers of Valley Forge were there, in an ultimate perspective, by their own choice. Men choose to wage wars. They choose to fight rather than negotiate. They choose to consider war realistic, and yielding unmanly and dangerous. To have assembled as an army, and then to insist that they be fed by those who did not wish their protection, presented ironies. If it were a matter of helping the poor and oppressed, the Mennonites were ready and willing. "We have dedicated ourselves" to such work, Bishop Benjamin Hershey had written. But to supply the food so that someone else was allowed to leave his own fields for the purpose of shedding his enemies' blood was another matter entirely.

The hungry men at Valley Forge, in the opinion of the defenseless Christians, would not need to be starving if they were at home. It was not the farmers, but themselves and their political cause that demanded the sacrifice. If the farmers sold them food, it was, practically speaking, an act supporting the war—a war they did not believe in and would have been extremely thankful to do without. If it were argued that they were shirking their duty, the answer is, their duty to whom? To the Congress that had been set up without their vote? To the New England and Virginia firebrands who had declared independence over their heads? To the soldiers who had the same option they had, of refusing to fight?

Here, as in all questions involving civil war and the much scarcer phenomenon of refusal to participate in any war because it is considered beneath the level of human beings created in the image of God, and foreign to the way of Christ's cross, the answer rides on the loyalties in the heart of the historian. Let it simply be said, after two

centuries of facile judgment of the farmers unwilling to
sell their butter, eggs, and cattle to a visiting army, that
they were the same simple people who could have saved
themselves vast sums of money had they taken up the
gun, or sworn the oath of allegiance like their neighbors.
Their actions are not reducible to mere economic
strategem.

There was, nonetheless, a kind of crassness in their
inability to take the war seriously. "Could not leave
home," noted a Lancaster County militia officer on his
roster next to the name of the "conscientiously scrupulous" Mennonite Jacob Hoover; "'twas seeding time."
The real needs of mankind had to be met, not the spurious lust for honor and the national egotisms that preoccupied the great men of power. The rhythms of God's
seasons were to be recognized, rather than the ebb and
flow of political rivalries. It had been thus for centuries already in the snug Bernese valleys.

Now Jacob and John Landis, petitioning from the
Lancaster jail, plead with the authorities to understand
that they are not "unfriendly to the States"; could not the
officers recognize country nonchalance? And Wendel
Bowman, having traveled from Lancaster County to
Philadelphia to fetch papers concerning the estate of his
recently deceased father, protests that he was only doing
his duty by his widowed mother, and has never in word or
deed acted against "the Honourable Congress." He cannot take the oath of allegiance, by which the officers tell
him his word would be accepted, because his conscience
"prohibits my taking an oath of enmity against any party
or individual whatsoever." But the hardheaded men of
this world, swearing to each other by the God who gave

His Son as a defenseless Lamb, consider such scruples to be at best pathetic baggage. In the real world which they control, defenseless Christians are an anomaly who are to be tolerated only to the point that the wars may proceed on schedule.

There are occasions when a defenseless Christian will risk her life. Among the corpses carried out of the soldiers' hospital at the Ephrata Cloister, three days before Wendel Bowman wrote his petition, was the wife of the Mennonite minister John Bear. A month later John too would succumb to the camp fever whose victims he and his wife had volunteered to nurse. Several of the valuable Cloister buildings eventually had to be burned to halt the virulent contagion.

As for Washington and his slowly recovering Army at Valley Forge, now being smartly drilled by the recently arrived Baron von Steuben, they cried out in ecstasy on May 6, "Huzza! Huzza! Huzza! Long live the king of France!" That, and the thunder of another *feu de joie* "swelling and rebounding from the neighboring hills, and gently sweeping along the Schuylkill," was sweeter music to a soldier's ear "than the most finished pieces of Handel." France was now allied with the Colonies, who could at last see victory clear after so much blood and uncertainty.

On May 18 the British Army, Lord Howe having been replaced, quietly pulled out of an apprehensive Philadelphia, and a day later Washington's confident troops pursued them in the direction of New York. Now that the American cause looked stronger, and the war itself had passed out of eastern Pennsylvania, some of its Whig citizens were eager to settle a few scores.

Chapter 10

The Great Calamity

The arrival of war in a community tests the bonds that hold it together. Old social wounds threaten to open, jealousies can no longer be hid, and defunct covenants are shown to be dead letters. If danger releases the best in some people, it triggers the worst in others. There is rifle-fire in the night, and bitter litigation by day.

Soldiers camping in unfamiliar counties are not uniformly tender for the feelings of their hosts. The liquor and sexual foraging by which they assuage their loneliness or shell-shock are accompanied by a host of lesser demoralizations. Thus little Moravian boys at Lititz were caught, by their parents, setting off "cartridges and powder" which they had gotten free from the many soldiers in the area by trading. Indignantly, one leader observed that they should buy nothing from the soldiers, if for no other reason than that what they had to sell was usually stolen. And why had the young schoolmaster bought from them a rifle? "What use has he, a schoolmaster, for a gun? He must be ordered to dispose of it."

Gradually, the war-pressure was sifting out the Moravian young men who were prepared to abandon their heritage of nonresistance. One of them, David Tanneberger, allowed himself to be elected a lieutenant in the militia, after which, though this automatically placed him out of the church, he refused to leave the community. His father was unable to help the church leaders, since he could exercise, he confessed, no authority over him. Another single member, Gottlieb Youngman, announced that he was leaving to enter the military, and although the leaders suggested that he go to Bethlehem first to discuss the move with his father, they "could do nothing with him, especially as he had previously, out of pure wantonness, taken the Oath of Allegiance." Twenty-one more of the Lititz group had sworn with him.

These Moravians had yielded the point when the Test Act had been harshly revised on April 1, 1778, so that refusing to take the oath after June 1 would cost considerably more than at first. In addition to the original penalties, persons still unwilling to take the oath would now be barred from making wills, would have to pay double their usual taxes, and be fined an extra ten pounds and costs or serve three months in jail. If none of these penalties worked, stubborn refusers could be exiled from the state within thirty days, and have their property confiscated.

Soon after this law had been intensified, Northampton County Lieutenant John Wetzel renewed his harassment of nonresistants in his territory. Among a group of men he had arrested were twelve Moravians from his home neighborhood in the region of Emmaus. Although the brotherhood had cared for many hundreds of sick and wounded soldiers at the risk of their lives, they were now accused of being unfriendly to the American cause. Having marched them in a procession through Bethlehem to the Easton jail, Wetzel swore that they were dangerous enemies of the state. It was claimed that one of them had fired at the constable who had been sent to arrest them, but this proved to have been the act of a non-Moravian neighbor. Spurious old stories about sending powder and shot to the Indians were dredged up. Finally all but one of the men were released, but a week later they were again called before a squire. The lone remaining prisoner, with whom Wetzel had a personal quarrel, appealed to the Supreme Court without success, and finally took the oath, paid the costs, and was released.

The new requirements seemed so outrageous, particularly the abjuration part, that Schwenkfelders joined with the Moravians to petition the Pennsylvania Assembly for relief. But the hardliners in the legislature stood rock-firm. "It cannot be conceived," one of them wrote, "that any person can bear allegiance to the United States of America, and at the same time refuse to renounce his allegiance to that power who, without any just pretense, is now carrying on an offensive and cruel war against us, laying waste, burning, plundering and destroying our country . . . and committing every outrage that refinement on savage barbarity can invent." Since "there are still some inhabitants who prefer slavery because of prejudice," it has become "necessary that distinction be made between friends and foes." The German-speaking Pennsylvanians should have no problem with the test oath, since when they were naturalized they had, as part of their promise of loyalty, renounced allegiance to a Royal

Family of England that had once been on the throne, and still "pretended" to it. Furthermore, since some Moravians had already taken the oath, the objections must be "of Individuals only," not the brotherhood as a whole.

This was the answer given for public consideration. Privately, the Executive Council wrote to Lieutenant Wetzel and asked him to cause less trouble over the matter. "These people are not to be feared," they noted, "either as to numbers or malice." Wetzel was not to call them especially to take the oath, or fine them more heavily than anyone else. Their refusal to cooperate in the war effort would cost them considerably, and if the government laid extra burdens on them, the citizenry would soon be talking of persecution. Basically, what the Assembly wished in these critical times was "to avoid any noises" from religious groups who were delinquent as to militia and tax obligations.

Shortly after these instructions were issued, a letter arrived in Philadelphia from a man who said he had heard "great complaints by Menonists and Quakers" in three counties, in regard to the oath. He suggested changing the wording to something they could in good conscience affirm, and the abolition of fines. A special tax should then be levied on them, he proposed, since they were known to believe in paying taxes.

Around this time another well-known nonresistant felt the brunt of the suspicions which mounted sharply just prior to the British pull-out from Philadelphia: editor-publisher Christopher Saur of Germantown. On May 8 he was ordered, with fifty-seven other citizens suspected of disloyalty, to present himself for swearing the oath.

Whereas his son, Christopher III, was actively aiding the British cause, the elder Saur remained neutral in deed; yet was considered among the enemies of the country. He returned to his home in Germantown, but was shortly routed from his bed at night by American soldiers, prodded through neighboring cornfields by bayonets, and kept overnight in a barn. In the morning he was stripped of his clothes, given an old shirt and breeches, painted black and red, and led barefoot and hatless toward Valley Forge, where the American Army still lingered. A friend who saw him in this condition asked the soldiers whether he might give Saur a pair of shoes. This was granted, but six miles further on another soldier took the shoes, giving Saur his "old slabs" in trade.

At Valley Forge the elderly printer was placed in the stockade, but the next morning General Peter Muhlenberg visited him and arranged for an appeal to Washington. A day later Saur was released, but with a pass that did not allow him to return to Germantown "during the stay of the enemy in this State." While he was waiting on the farm of a nearby Dunkard, new regulations regarding those suspected of Toryism were published, including instructions to enter special bail in the courts, but Christopher did not hear of them, isolated as he was.

The bitterness of the times was now seeping into the life of the Franconia Mennonites, through the crack provided by the formidable ego of their Bishop Christian Funk. As in the case of the Lancaster Bishop Martin Boehm, who had become a kind of Mennonite Methodist, a vigorous leader was beginning to espouse ideas from sources beyond his own tradition, and the guardians of the heritage were stiffening their resistance. They sensed, almost inarticulately, what could be contained within the inherited patterns of church life, and what would prove impossible, in time, to control. Bishop Funk's egregious opinions regarding the payment of fines and his favorable attitude toward the Congress were common knowledge, and the cause of critical gossip. Although there were people on both sides of the fine question in his Indianfield congregation, all of the ministers and deacons disagreed with their bishop. Jacob Oberholtzer, on the next farm, was to become the spokesman for members who disapproved of Christian's attitude, his way of managing his business affairs, and his conduct of his household.

Christian was unaware of the impending great calamity—the breakdown of his authority in the congregations at Indianfield (Franconia), Bechtel's (Rockhill), Clemens' (Salford), and Plains. The discontent suddenly surfaced as he was preparing for the annual communion services. From the beginnings of the Anabaptist movement the Lord's Supper had been held among the people now called Mennonites only after exceptionally careful soul-searching, and inquiry among the congregation as to whether all members were at peace with their brothers and sisters. Without this, Mennonites believed, the Supper would be an empty symbol. Sometimes there was considerable reconciliation to be accomplished, and the Supper had to be postponed until peace was established. That, however, was the exception.

Having invited the eight ministers and deacons from his congregations to discuss the approaching communion, Christian began by expressing his own peace and readiness to proceed. To his surprise there was a negative response from his elderly but still vigorous uncle, Deacon

Christian Meyer: "I cannot break the bread at this time. I am not satisfied with myself." This was echoed by similar sentiments from each of the other seven ordained men. "If this is the case," responded Bishop Funk crisply, "you may all leave and go home. If you aren't fit to break the bread you aren't fit to preach."

It then became evident that the others were willing to proceed if it came to that, but that Deacon Meyer was not. With this point clarified, plans were made to interrogate the membership of each congregation in a preparatory counsel meeting, to determine whether the communion might fittingly be held. A Sunday for such a meeting was set, but before it arrived one of the Rockhill ministers, Samuel Bechtel (who had bought bishop Isaac Kolb's farm when the latter had moved to Plains), stated his opinion to Bishop Funk that those who polled the congregations, to take their sentiments, should not be ministers. This was a departure from tradition, and an obvious hint that Funk's leadership was not fully trusted. When the poll was taken Christian found no problems at Salford, but fourteen persons expressed dissatisfaction in Bechtel's congregation at Rockhill.

On the following Tuesday evening the bishop's fellow minister Jacob Oberholtzer and Deacon Henry Rosenberger came to his mill-farm and stated that since every member had expressed peace toward everyone but their own bishop, Christian would not be able to proceed with the annual Lord's Supper. Christian demanded to know the content of the complaints, but his visitors refused to divulge them. This irritated Christian's wife, Barbara, and she burst out that they had a habit of "creating contentions before the breaking of bread." Angrily,

Jacob Oberholtzer replied that he could tell her of a hundred sins of her husband, and the two visitors left abruptly.

This was serious business. Early the next morning the bishop traveled up the creek that powered his mill, past Jacob Oberholtzer's home to the next farm, where Deacon Henry Rosenberger lived. He insisted that the Deacon tell him who his fourteen accusers at Rockhill were, and was directed to ask the Rockhill Deacon, miller Isaac Derstine. Isaac revealed the names of fourteen persons. Christian immediately went to their homes and found that the basis of their dissatisfaction was the report that he had "allowed" the payment of the three pounds ten shillings fine, which Christian referred to as a tax, and that he had not expressed disapproval of the upstart Continental Congress. His explanations appeared to satisfy all but the wives of the two Rockhill ministers, who were mother and daughter. Mrs. Samuel Bechtel replied indignantly to the bishop's questions that her Reformed neighbors, "the Hartzells," had stated flatly that Christian had taken the test oath, contrary to traditional Mennonite practice. Christian calmly denied this, and asked whether it was not shameful to make unfounded accusations against ministers. Tearfully, Mrs. Bechtel and her daughter Elizabeth Gehman then expressed their peace with the bishop.

Christian at once called on his neighbor Jacob Oberholtzer, to inform him that everyone else but Jacob and Deacon Rosenberger had now expressed peace, and that it looked as though the Supper would be held as usual. He asked Jacob how he felt about the angry words that had passed between him and Barbara Funk on the previous Tuesday night. "Go home and tell your wife," confessed Jacob, "that I was in a passion that evening." When Deacon Rosenberger likewise expressed a readiness to overlook the disagreement, plans for communion were completed, and to the apparent satisfaction of the congregations "a large supper was held."

However, while Christian was confined to his home by sickness immediately after the day of communion, his fellow ministers again raised the issue of paying the "tax" of three pounds ten shillings. Although the congregation had people on both sides of the issue, the ministers once again called on them to withhold the tax. Then, as Christian was recuperating, he was visited by his fellow bishop from the other side of Salford, saddler Andrew Ziegler. Andrew informed the miller that his uncle Christian Meyer and Andrew had recently proposed, in the Mennonite community at Hereford, that no Mennonite should pay the tax. Unaware as yet of the depth of Andrew's feelings on the topic, Christian replied, "I think we can pay it." But a short time later, as the two bishops were meeting with another—elderly, weak-sighted Abraham Schwartz of Bedminster Township—Christian heard Andrew Ziegler state decisively, "We can not pay the three pounds ten shillings tax."

Still underestimating the great calamity of unbrotherliness that was to curse the rest of his life, Christian found Bishop Ziegler approaching his home one day in the company of six ministers. As was customary, Christian stepped forward to greet them with a kiss of peace, only to see Andrew draw back sharply, saying, "I won't give you the kiss." The other brethren followed suit.

"Has the matter become as bad as that?" queried

Christian. "You may, though, come into the house."

Having sat down, Andrew stated that they had come to determine whether it was permissible for their people, as defenseless Christians, to pay the tax.

"You already know my opinion," replied Christian, very much dissatisfied by what he considered their "unevangelical" manner of denying him the brotherly greeting. Andrew then asked him how paying the tax could be seen as permissible "according to the gospel." Christian replied that the Jews, in Christ's time, had not considered Caesar to be their legitimate ruler, and yet had been instructed by Christ to pay the taxes Caesar demanded.

"If Christ were here," Christian went on, "he would say, 'Give unto *Congress* that which belongs to Congress, and to God what is God's.' "

Deeply displeased, Andrew Ziegler rose from his seat and said (if Christian's quotation is accurate) that if it weren't for the added factor of danger, there would be no difference between going to war and paying the tax by which the war was supported. Andrew then left in anger, according to Christian.

The majority if not all of the ministers believed, in Christian's opinion, that the British might still win the war. He considered this to be their main reason for objecting to both fines and oath, and he felt that this was a "backward" outlook. On the other hand, his fellow ministers and bishops considered him and some of his relatives as headstrong and uncooperative, and could not imagine how they could repudiate their earlier promises of loyalty to the British king. They were far from alone in their position, but, unlike many other Loyalists, they were prepared neither to fight against the king's op-

ponents nor to leave the country. Under the leadership of
Bishop Ziegler they now decided to silence their Whig-
minded leader, as his brother Henry had been silenced
several years earlier, denying him the right to preach and
administer the ordinances of communion or baptism.

Christian ignored this, on the advice, as he said, of
"twenty of the oldest brethren," and preached as usual on
the following Sunday, no other minister appearing at
the meetinghouse he attended. A week later Jacob
Oberholtzer rose behind the pulpit and conducted the
meeting. On the third Sunday Christian went to Indianfield, and joined the other ministers in the little room
where they consulted before the meeting. The ministers
appeared indifferent to his arrival, and left him standing
alone while they went out and conferred beside the
graveyard wall. Christian then walked into the pulpit, but
as soon as the singing was over, one of the other ministers
immediately got up to "make the opening," and another
followed him without a pause. Christian thus had no
chance to speak, and on his way home was told by a sympathetic brother, "These men have stolen the word from
you today."

When Bishops Andrew Ziegler and Abraham Schwartz
(the latter in his late seventies and eventually forced by
blindness to let someone else read his text before he
preached) showed up at Indianfield on the sixth Sunday,
Christian knew that something special was brewing. In
the course of the sermon, with Christian sitting beside
them, the bishops used such texts as, "Except thou repent
I will remove the candlestick out of its place" —clearly referring to a forthcoming deposition of the bishop.

From his side of the matter, Christian viewed himself

as a prophet with an unpopular message—like Jeremiah, who had told his people that they were about to lose a war. But the Bishops Ziegler and Schwartz now moved to complete his silencing. Calling together forty men from the Indianfield congregation to meet with the eight local ministers and deacons, they charged Christian with losing his colleagues' respect for the management of his "house," having poor relations with his congregation, and suspicion of having taken the test oath. They further informed him that any person who "adheres to Congress or even inclines that way" should have nothing to say in their deliberations.

Harsher criticism lay in store for Christian, as gossip made the rounds that he had told at least two of the younger men in the congregation that they might as well take the test oath and save themselves the ten-pound fine. Whenever he denied that he himself had taken the oath, someone reported hearing from non-Mennonite sources that he had, and that he had even shown people his certificate for it. Shady business dealings were attributed to him. Christian stood pretty much alone, now, except for his brother Henry, miller at Hosensack. He too was being forced by unpopularity within the brotherhood to review his earlier opposition to the oath. Lieutenant John Wetzel was seeking to force him to pay two militia fines totaling over ninety pounds. Wetzel argued that Henry could not claim a minister's exemption from the militia, since he was no longer recognized as a minister by his own group. This seemed unfair to Henry, who continued to act as a leader in the Mennonite community even though he had been silenced. In one case he appealed on behalf of Abraham and Michael Meyer, when the local militia officials sought to confiscate their property because of their nonresistant stand.

Farsighted as Henry's brother Christian may have been politically, a more diplomatic spirit would have gone a long way toward eliminating the troubles in which he was increasingly embroiled. But he apparently could not say, as Lutheran Pastor Muhlenberg wrote, "I have no vocation to meddle in political controversy." The Lutheran patriarch too had discovered how difficult it was, as he put it, "for upright preachers to exist between . . . embittered contending parties." He attributed the collapse of neighborliness to the unruliness released by the war-spirit. "Small, narrow, and short-sighted fellows" now come out of the cracks where they have hidden. In the current atmosphere of suspicion "the basest man can ruin an innocent acquaintance whom he does not like. All that is necessary is that he point with his finger and whisper in someone's ear, 'That man is a rebel or this man is a Tory,' and revenge and ruin will follow without impartial investigation, judgment, and legal procedure. In such short trials, moreover, the stronger man is usually right and the weaker must pay the costs."

That the pastor was not exaggerating was abundantly proven in the summer of 1778, in the sad experience of the Mennonite congregation at Saucon, several miles south of Bethlehem. Their troubles arose when the stringent new rules of the second Test Act were applied by the local militia officers, who had been appointed agents for the forfeit of estates by persons attainted of treason. "In times like these," to use Pastor Muhlenberg's words, "envious persons and enemies who at other times would be secret, rise up as accusers and vent their petty rage because they never had a chance to do it before." A number of such persons flourished at and soon after the withdrawal of the British from Philadelphia, when attention could be diverted to punishing those who had cooperated with, or, in some cases, actively aided the British cause. In the quest for revenge on such people suspicion sometimes ranked as proof, and the innocent were occasionally victimized. One elderly Quaker miller from Upper Merion Township was hanged, despite a petition signed by 4,000 people, as was a farmer from Hatfield Township. Before the latter was executed, several of his Mennonite neighbors, with a number of Welsh Quakers, signed a fruitless petition for his pardon, citing the plight of his wife and several small children. Many confiscations of property and real estate took place, as officials eager to settle old scores and collect a percentage of the price brought by sheriff's auctions did their work.

On the day before the British departure, a dozen Mennonite men were hailed into court at Easton by two justices of the peace, one of whom was Squire Frederick Limbach, and requested to prove their colors by taking the test oath. All but one were married, and most were farmers, with one blacksmith, Henry Geissinger, among them. In their community, with the apparent allowance of their bishop, Jacob Meyer, they had paid both taxes and fines to the new government, "furnished horses and teams for the continental service whenever demanded," and occasionally gone along with their teams as drivers. But on the test oath they were as unyielding as they were on taking up arms: it was contrary to their principles "in any case whatever." Though they were informed of the requirements of the new law, they insisted that they were

not "able yet to get over their religious scruples." Taking
the test appeared to them, they claimed, "like joining our
hands to the military service."

The Northampton County magistrates felt not the
slightest sympathy for a position they were trying to
eradicate in their district. To their astonishment, the
Mennonite farmers heard themselves sentenced to be
banished from the state within thirty days, with all their
personal property except their real estate to be confiscated and sold by the sheriff. Their former peaceful behavior, the pregnancy of several of their wives, and their
lack of ill-will toward the new government were all dismissed as mitigating factors.

It remained difficult for the Mennonites to believe that
the militia officers appointed to the task would actually
carry it out, but on June 24 two men arrived on the farms
of Abraham Geissinger and Henry and Peter Sell to take
an inventory. It was already a dark day for the Mennonite
community, when an eclipse of the sun occurred in fitting
symbolism of their gloom. Over the next few days the
other farms were visited, and their animals, tools, house
furniture, and utensils cataloged. Even the iron stoves,
though bolted to the floor, went into the account. Only
the uncut hay and standing grain in the fields were unin-
ventoried.

In alarm the convicted men appealed, on July 4, 1778,
directly to the Supreme Executive Council of Pennsylvania. They protested "in all humility" that their
sentence had been pronounced for no other reason than
their obeying their religious scruples against the test, and
asked the council to rectify the magistrate's error, which
arose, they suggested, from a misreading of the law. With

the appeal went a statement signed by twelve neighbors of the Mennonite families, describing the accused men as having an "unblemished reputation for uprightness and integrity," and blaming "their present blindness to their own Essential interests" on "an unhappy bias in their Education," rather than disloyalty.

While the Saucon congregation hoped anxiously for clemency from higher authorities, other people were feeling equal heat from the Test Act. Christopher Saur, Jr., whose son had been printing for the British and now had actually left with them and was trying to agitate the German populace against the Revolutionary cause, had only been back at his Germantown home for a month when two colonels came and asked whether he had taken out the new special bail with the Supreme Court. He replied that he had been unaware of any law requiring this. They then asked whether he had taken the test oath.

"No," replied the printer.

"Why not? Were you so attached to the king?"

"No," Christopher explained; "it was not the attachment to the king. You have in your Act that they that do not take that oath shall not have a right to buy nor sell." This was so close to the prediction in the Book of Revelation of an evil "mark of the beast," that Christian said he "could not take that oath while it stood on that condition."

"But you went to the English, to Philadelphia," said Colonel Smith accusingly.

"Do you know why?"

"No, nor do I want to know."

At this point the officers informed Saur that the purpose of their call was to take an inventory of his property,

prior to confiscation for selling it at auction. One of them
stood guard to keep the old printer from removing anything while the other went for an appraiser. They listed his
medicines, the use of which only he understood, his bed,
and even a barrel of rice. Finally he asked if he could keep
his spectacles, which was granted. In spite of his frantic
efforts to get the auction stopped by appeals to other authorities, he was sold out to the bare walls, and his house
was rented out and later sold.

The Test Act controversy also disrupted the life of
Welsh Baptists in the vicinity of Hilltown Township, adjacent to Franconia. The Whig-Tory split had invaded
their fellowship, and some, though they were not pacifists, had refused to take the oath. Technically, this
meant that they could not travel outside of their county.
To their angry disgust they found themselves arrested
when crossing the Bucks-Philadelphia county line on
their way to church in Montgomery Township, and taken
before a justice of the peace who was a member of their
own congregation. He saw that the accusations were
based on petty hatreds, released his fellow Baptists, and
announced that there should be no more such arrests. The
harassment rankled so sorely, however, that before the
war had ended there was a separation, and fifty-four
members began a new church in Hilltown.

Two Franconia Mennonites who were remembered to
have taken provisions to Philadelphia while the British
were there now had a warrant issued for their arrest. One
of the charges indicated that they had still refused to take
the oath of allegiance. One of them, John Souder, would
marry the stepdaughter of preacher Jacob Funk of Germantown.

By the end of August, time had run out for the Saucon Mennonites, and no relief had been granted by the state government. Sheriff John Siegfried supervised a "Publick Vendue" at which the movable goods of George Bachman were sold to the highest bidder. Members and relatives of the Bachman family managed to buy twenty-six of fifty-six lots of their own goods, including the clock for seventy-five pounds and all the furniture except one bed, the spinning wheel, and some hogs and sheep, but none of the cows or horses. On the same day a larger sale was held disposing of the goods of Caspar Yoder. Here the only Mennonite buyer was John Bare, who got the Bible. The pacifist-hater Squire Limbach was on hand, and bought himself "a hand screw."

So it went for the next ten days, until 40,000 pounds worth of farm and household goods had been sold for the support of the war and the punishment of traitors. At one of the sales Sheriff Siegfried himself bought the large Bible, a chair, two beds, books, and a hand screw. Three other parcels of books were sold from the same home— Jacob Yoder's. Doubtless among them was the *Ausbund*, an American reprint of the Mennonite hymnbook containing ballads and accounts of jailings, confiscations, and executions suffered by the ancestors of these peaceful farmers in the old country. A list of the Yoders' worldly goods passing into the hands of their neighbors evokes the flavor of their life: churn, spinning wheel, walnut table, scythe, sickles, chisels, currycomb, augers, cow chains, ax, saw, shovel, rakes, leather and wool, harrow, plows, hayforks, clock, and two stoves. Finally, on September 3, the corner cupboard of the Abraham Yoders, the large spinning wheel and looking glass of Christian Young, and

the cattle of both farms "mixed together by the carelessness of the drivers" were auctioned off with Henry Geissinger's blacksmith tools, and the law protecting Pennsylvania from traitors had taken its course. Now, in addition
to their unfurnished houses and the clothes on their
backs, all that the families of the jailed men owned was
the standing hay and grain in their fields.

Six days later an anguished petition, signed with the
marks of Eve Yoder and Esther Bachman, wives of two of
the imprisoned farmers, was sent to the Pennsylvania
Assembly in Philadelphia. It rehearsed the pathetic
details of the justice Northampton County had exacted
from the harmless Mennonites. "From some of them,"
read the plaint, "all their provisions were taken and not
even a morsel of bread left them for their children." Since
all their iron stoves were taken from them, though
fastened to the floors, "they are deprived of every means
of keeping their children warm in the approaching
winter, especially at nights, being obliged to sleep on the
floor without any beds." The women begged the
Assembly to mitigate the severity of the sentence, to allow
their husbands "to dwell with" them again, and not to
take their children from them. They reminded the legislators of the command in the Scriptures, "What God hath
joined together let not man put asunder."

The Assembly, after hearing the petition, asked for a
quick investigation of the facts, with the request that if
they were found to be true, money should be taken from
the state treasury to relieve these Mennonite victims of
overzealous patriots. Three men who looked into the matter reported that Abraham Geissinger's wife had indeed
"not a bed left her although she was near the time of de-

livery," and also was one of the most needy in the group. Henry Sell, shortly before his goods were seized, had also been robbed of his cash, and was now "at some times somewhat delirious." By what the committee could learn, the crops that had been gathered after the seizure would last the petitioners for a year, and they estimated the loss at only one fourth of what the goods had actually brought at the auctions.

Such tardy and fragmentary inquiry doubtless did little to alleviate the stings of the loss of painfully collected family possessions, but it fell far short of the crowning irony which was to mark the memories of Jacob Yoder, John Geissinger, and their friends who sacrificed all they had to separate themselves from the Revolutionary War for conscience' sake. For all their pains, their graves are yearly marked with American flags placed by modern patriotic organizations, who, having carelessly read the rosters of Colonel Siegfried's militia, in their myth-making zeal designate these defenseless, dispossessed Christians as soldier heroes of the American Revolution.

Chapter 11

The Painful Coming of Peace

Although the war had largely passed from Pennsylvania soil by the harvest of 1778, its mark remained deeply stamped on town and country. No one was completely untouched, in soul if not in body. Joseph Fretz had saved his fine horse from some of Washington's soldiers, but his cousin Elizabeth lost her heart to another one of them, young John Kephart of Philadelphia. In time he would espouse his wife's humble faith, and, the Revolution having ended thirteen years earlier, be ordained a nonresistant Mennonite minister at the meeting near Doylestown.

The aging Deacon Christian Meyer had lost one of his two capable minister-sons to the "yellow fever" that had killed off so many soldiers during the previous year, and shortly after Jacob had died, his wife had been taken by the same deadly malady. Christian's other son Samuel, at forty-four, was a well-respected minister in the same district; his daughter Fronica had married young Abraham Wismer, back from his carting for the American Army. Of considerable concern was the health of a third son of Deacon Meyer, Christian, III, now approaching fifty and still within draft age. His grandfather's farm at Indianfield had passed into his care, but now the elderly deacon had to travel to the inn in nearby Lower Salford, where the local militia companies convened, and report to Captain Campbell that Christian, III, was so sickly that he could not report on mustering day, let alone work to pay off his fine. This was perhaps questionable in light of Christian, III's, ownership of the original Meyer 232-acre homestead, with, as recently as five years earlier, five horses and seven cows.

The many nonresistants in Franconia and adjacent Lower Salford continued to pay enormous amounts, in the inflated Continental currency, for their non-participation throughout the war. However, when they felt they had legitimate reasons to be excused from mustering, they appealed, just as their nonpacifist neighbors did, to have their fines remitted as well. Michael Ziegler, who satisfied his captain that he was "very lame," paid less than one third of the normal fine. Garret Godshalk was "reported by his Neighbors" to be "troubled with the fitts," and was therefore discharged on one occasion. Benjamin Hendricks was required to pay "three fourths of his fines" even though he pleaded that he had had bad luck with his animals, had "a large helpless family," and was "Elderly and weakly." Leonard Hendricks tried to plead that he was "afraid to turn out for fear some others might make company with" his sickly wife "in his absence," but was not excused.

John Detweiler, son-in-law of Christian Funk, pleaded vainly that he could not spare his son at home, while

Christian and Isaac Bergey had "sore legs." Deacon
Meyer's son-in-law Martin Detweiler was charged one
fourth less than usual on one occasion because he was
"unwell," while John Rosenberger and John Clemens,
both of whom had recently married, were also given a
lower rate as "new beginners." Isaac Kratz's neighbors
testified that the rheumatism in his legs was sometimes so
bad that he could not get out of bed, but he was nevertheless required to pay half his fine. Miller John Alderfer
along Branch Creek produced a doctor's certificate "setting forth that he has got the Ague." More intriguing
were the pleas of young men like John's brother Joseph,
husband of another of Deacon Meyer's granddaughters,
that the land they lived on did not really belong to them.

Joseph, not quite thirty, and his wife Maria were child-
less. His father, the now wealthy immigrant Friedrich
Altdörfer who had married the widow of his Mennonite
employer and joined her nonresistant church, had legally
transferred the Alderfer homestead to Joseph three days
before the Declaration of Independence. The same thing
had been done with the Alderfer mill, taken over by
Joseph's brother John. Apparently Joseph claimed in his
appeal that the money for this purchase remained to be
paid, though the deed was already in his name.

Thus the Mennonites, like everyone else, sought ways
to evade the unwelcome levies made upon them by the
troubled new government. Joseph Alderfer's Lowe Salford neighbors did not regard him as non-public spirited,
for they had appointed him along with his rheumatism-
plagued Mennonite neighbor Isaac Kratz as "overseers of
the poor" in the township two years earlier.

In the midst and doubtless because of the current difficulties with their bishop, the congregation at Indianfield had now ordained yet another preacher, 21-year-old John Bergey. This youthful addition to the team raised the total of ordained servants of the congregation to five: Bishop Funk, Ministers Bergey and Oberholtzer, and Deacons Meyer and Rosenberger.

Christian Funk, who had the superior office, was becoming increasingly resented by the other four leaders as he refused to work along with their opposition to the test oath. As an older man, Christian's uncle Deacon Meyer also had considerable authority; he was treasurer of the alms, and a confirmed deacon. This made him responsible for visiting and admonishing members who had, in some way, broken the covenant of the church. Observing increasing tension in the congregation as their bishop was being brought under open criticism, Meyer was displeased to hear his nephew nevertheless announce one Sunday morning in meeting that those who desired baptism should meet the following Sunday afternoon to begin a class of instruction. Such a move assumed that the congregation was willing to allow a bishop to function who, it was rumored, not only had signed his own oath certificate, but had advised others to do so, counter to the express wish of his fellow ministers and bishops. Though he had denied it publicly, the rumors would not go away, and now the other bishops had wished him to be silenced.

The Brethren (Dunkards) were struggling with the same issues and had declared after much reflection in their yearly meeting that their members who had taken the oath should be asked to recall it before a justice, acknowledge their error in their churches, and truly repent. If they refused to do this they would have to be "deprived of the kiss of fellowship" and the Lord's Supper until they would become obedient again. If ministers or bishops (elders) had taken the oath, and were now willing to recall it, counsel should be held as to whether they might again serve in their office, but such as might defend their action stubbornly would be considered unfit to serve in the Lord's vineyard. They would be regarded, further, as unfit even to be members in the church. The declaration closed with the agonizing prayer, "May God have mercy upon us!" A year later this position was reiterated: since it is impossible to know yet "whether God has rejected the king and chosen the state," those who have already taken it upon themselves to cast off the king's authority by accepting the oath cannot have done right. Ministers who have done so must stop functioning in their office, and if they persist, they must be deprived of "the church council and the holy kiss" of peace.

Although the Mennonite position was similar, here was Bishop Funk who presumed to convene his congregations for the Lord's Supper, and now to baptize. His uncle Christian Meyer dragged his feet until the actual time was set for baptism, and then told the bishop that two of the applicants should not be received. When he was asked why, he replied perfunctorily that they were not in harmony with the Word. His nephew then insisted that they visit the two applicants together for an examination, which forced Deacon Meyer to admit that he had really come to tell the bishop that he would not cooperate in the baptism; that is, he would not bring water, as the deacons were expected to do for a baptism. Rather, he told his nephew, what was needed was for him to make peace with his offended fellow ministers. The younger man replied that no one else was hindering him except the other deacon, Henry Rosenberger, who had likewise said he would bring no water. As Meyer prepared to leave, the bishop offered him the traditional kiss, but the older man drew back.

"Are you not in peace?" demanded Funk.

"Are you?" returned his uncle, and left.

The bishop then proceeded on his own to interview the two (of nineteen) applicants rejected by his uncle, and prepared to baptize them. After the deacon from the Plains meeting had also refused to bring water, Christian was faced with the choice of resigning, campaigning against his fellow ministers, or going ahead somehow as though nothing had happened. After speaking with several friends, he took the unsanctioned step of having his unordained brother, John, perform the service of the deacon. The baptisms, water having at last been unofficially brought, were carried out at Franconia.

This was too much. Christian Meyer informed Barbara Funk that she and her bishop husband could expect visitors on the following Wednesday. On the appointed day, with Froene Funk, Christian's sister, at their side, the bishop and his wife received the delegation: Christian Meyer, Deacon Henry Rosenberger, young John Bergey, and Minister Abraham Gehman from Rockhill, son-in-law of the older minister there, Samuel Bechtel. Of the Indianfield leadership, only Jacob Oberholtzer was absent. Refusing the kiss, they sat down, and John Bergey explained their visit.

"It is because it goes so bad in the congregation," the recently ordained minister began. "You pursue your course too obstinately, and have attached yourself to the

wicked world. You have given two sermons which were
not according to the gospel, in which you criticized an innocent man [neighbor Jacob Oberholtzer]. You said, to be
sure, that you had no particular person in mind." In brief,
John said, "We have come to inform you that we consider
you unfit to exercise your functions until you sincerely
repent."

At last the challenge had been openly delivered.

"And what have I done?" demanded the bishop.

"You have tried to make Jacob Oberholtzer a liar."

Funk then said that he had offered peace to his
neighbor and fellow minister.

"Yes," replied young Bergey, "with your lips, but not
with your heart."

This was more disrespect than Froene Funk could
stand to see offered her bishop brother by a young minister less than half his age. "Do you make a man a liar
before his face?" she asked.

"We are not making him a liar."

"But you won't allow anything he says to carry any
weight."

As it became clear that the ministers had already
reached a firm decision against Christian while meeting
previously in Deacon Meyer's home, the bishop became
indignant. He claimed that they were maneuvering
around him on a "non-evangelical" basis. When young
Minister Bergey said that he had been told through a justice of the peace that the bishop had not only taken the
oath but showed his certificate to the justice, Christian
snapped back, "These are your rotten lies; you have no
other evidence. I can not submit to your judgment."

Thus ended the unhappy interview at which Christian

Funk's official ministry was repudiated. Now that he had clearly stated his unwillingness to take the counsel of the church, and was looking for support among his relatives (only three of whom, at first, approved his actions), the two bishops of the neighboring districts were called in again. Andrew Ziegler and the weak-eyed Abraham Schwartz convened a special meeting of the men of the Indianfield congregation, and began by having the ministers gather in the small room apart from the other members. Here they told Bishop Funk that his congregation had raised three complaints against him: his management of his household, his administration of the church, and his favoring of the allegiance to a government which had appointed itself to overthrow the king. Christian responded that he was not receiving a proper hearing, and that the other bishops should direct his fellow ministers to be reconciled with him.

"Then," observed his cousin Jacob, minister at Germantown, and slowly recovering from the severe losses of the war, "you would have things as you see them. Have you submitted to the congregation?"

That, after all, was the key point in traditional Mennonite life, growing out of the original teaching on yieldedness. Once the rebellious, individualistic American spirit had entered the congregation, allowing members to make up their own minds in regard to political or economic issues, even in opposition to the brotherhood, something basic had changed. It was one thing to have opinions. But when one rammed them through the brotherhood because one felt one was clearer-minded on current events, there could be no covenant.

On the other hand, Christian Funk's irritated response to the accusations about which he had not been consulted before they had been made public was understandable. The ironclad authority of a nondemocratic tradition left little room for consideration of fresh alternatives. Now the bishops insisted, against Christian's wishes, on going from their little room to where the congregation sat waiting to hear the charges against their Whiggish leader. Sixty-two men listened as Andrew Ziegler began, "Whoever has taken the allegiance shall have nothing to say here."

Apparently accepting these conditions, Bishop Funk asked that his accusers speak first. His uncle Meyer made a few remarks, and then Minister Jacob Oberholtzer, protesting that he was no accuser, poured out a flood of criticisms, showing how the tensions had built up a backlog of ill feeling in which the issues of the Revolution had become intertwined with personal grievance.

"I . . . say," began Oberholtzer, "that Christian Funk and his children are very proud and obstinate. If they are spoken to, they disregard it, and if he is told of this, he replies, 'Talk to them; they'll be sure to send you home.' If Christian Funk happens to be at another meeting, on his return he asks his children who preached at home, and when they say Jacob Oberholtzer or John Bergey, he asks what text was used, and then they laugh and ridicule us. They quote the proverb [in reference to Jacob Oberholtzer and John Bergey] 'The Lord is like the servant and the servant like the Lord.' He has encouraged [three neighbors] to take the affirmation of allegiance. . . . If we were to manage our affairs as he does we would have to tear several pages out of the gospel."

It was developing into a shabby, unpleasant evening in the life of the church. Bishop Funk, protesting that none of the charges were true, and that this was the first he had heard of any of them, was taken back into the chamber, and informed that twenty persons had submitted complaints against him. He was now deliberately asked by Bishops Ziegler and Schwartz to "submit to the common council." He refused, stating that since false witness had been given, he could not submit without a fairer examination. If he could be convinced that he had transgressed according to gospel standards, he said, he would acknowledge his error.

"You must oppose the allegiance," replied the bishops.

This backward step the bishop could not bring himself to take. "I will leave that to another time," was his ambiguous response. The other bishops' reaction was to turn to the waiting congregation and announce "that Christian Funk did not submit himself to the council." Standing outside the door now in the darkness, Christian was advised by several supporters to go home. "You see how falsely and unjustly they accuse you," one said. Christian replied that he would rather go with the congregation. There had never been a rupture among the Franconia Mennonites. They were all closely intermarried, knew each other's business, and were called by their confession to live in love. Finally, against his friends' advice, Christian walked back into the meetinghouse, stood before the table, and asked the pardon of anyone in the congregation whom he might have offended in any way. He asked them to pray for him, as he would for them, and to have patience once more.

"That is not the thing," replied one of the other

leaders. "You must oppose the taking of the allegiance."

"I am innocent of that," insisted Christian, and refused any further concession. The impasse was now definite. He was told that he was to stop preaching until he had changed his mind, and the meeting was dismissed. A later gathering, held without Christian's knowledge, took the final drastic step of declaring that he was to be treated, in regard to church life, as a heathen and a publican, since he was no longer willing to accept the council of the brethren. Bishops Andrew Ziegler, Jacob Meyer, and Philip Geissinger, the latter two from the Great Meadow (Swamp) districts where they had silenced Henry Funk, now informed Christian officially that he was no longer in communion with his congregation. Christian angrily told them that they ought to be ashamed before God and man to excommunicate him without a proper investigation of the charges.

Feeling increasingly isolated, the bishop visited two Mennonite leaders along the Schuylkill River, some fifteen miles to the west. Neither Martin Bechtel, owner of a ferry, nor his neighbor Jacob Knorr was willing to interfere in the business of their fellow bishops to the east. Christian then wrote a passionately detailed account of the whole affair for the perusal of the Mennonites of Lancaster County, only to find, eventually, that they regarded it as a scandalous book, unnecessarily showing "other people . . . what passes among us." Unfavorable rumors of his business dealings now multiplied, and Christian heard bits of gossip drifting back from Philadelphia, to which the farmers were again free to take their produce. It was claimed that he had given wormy meal in exchange for good, had cheated Franconia Township out of twenty-five pounds in a horse deal, and taken rams from the flocks of both his uncle Christian Meyer and his fellow Minister Jacob Oberholtzer.

As Christian's brothers and sisters, sons-in-law, children and friends were drawn into the controversy, most of them took his part, claiming that he was being treated unjustly. His brother Henry was now called by Christian to preach "with and for him," as Henry's disapproving neighbors put it. The Hosensack miller was reported at last to have taken the oath, under the severe pressures of local justices. A group began meeting with the Funks on the Sundays when there was no regular gathering in the Indianfield meetinghouse. Shortly thereafter several men, including Christian's neighbor George Delp, "put a lock on the door and . . . stood guard on Sunday." Christian sent two men to beg admittance for them, since, as he claimed, "it was ours and our fathers' inheritance," but entrance was refused, and the Funkites now met first outdoors, and then in houses and barns. The rupture was complete.

In the meantime, the state had temporarily softened the penalties of the Test Act, after receiving new petitions from nonresistant people. The Moravians at Lititz responded to the news "with joy and thankfulness," noting that although those who were excused from the oath for reasons of conscience would not be allowed to vote, hold public office, or serve on a jury, these were privileges which they had "never troubled ourselves about" anyway.

As for miller Henry Funk, now with his brother Christian no longer allowed to preach in the regular Mennonite meetings, taking the allegiance had only complicated his

position. The pacifist-baiter Squire Limbach was still harassing him, claiming that since he had been expelled
from the Mennonite society he could no longer hope to be
excused as a minister from fines for neglect of militia
duty. Under repeated instructions from the government
the squire had refrained from levying fines on law-abid-
ing nonresistants, but he saw here a technicality whereby
he could keep pressure on miller Funk.

Henry went to see Daniel Hiester of Sumneytown,
Colonel of the local battalion of the militia, to ask for
relief. The Colonel had seen much of the bitterness of
war, having spent months recently in Nova Scotia trying
to help his wayward young brother-in-law who had been
taken prisoner by the British. During his visit he had finally gotten the youthful John Hager to sign a deed
which had placed the site of future Hagerstown, Maryland, in the Colonel's ownership. He was now a man of
considerable means and influence, and he was above partisan meanness. He listened to Henry Funk's complaint,
and sat down to write a recommendation for Henry to
take to a member of the Council of Safety. "I know," he
wrote, that "he and his brother Christian Funk (a
remarkably strong Whig), are preaching to the few well
affected of that society," and that "he is a man of good
character." There really had been no reason, observed
the Colonel, for reading him out of the Mennonite fellowship, except "his attachment to the cause of this country."
Hiester added that it seemed strange for Limbach to pe-
nalize a man for "complying with the Law of his country
[i.e., taking the oath], simply" because he is disowned by
his own religious group.

Eventually Henry Funk's appeal reached a committee

of three American generals. Whether or not his penalties were withdrawn, he was no longer content to remain in a community where he was in difficulty both within and without his church. He sold his mill to George Kriebel, with whom he had been jailed for at first refusing the oath. Three years after the war closed he moved with most of his family to the Shenandoah Valley of Virginia, where his son Joseph, born in the midst of his troubles at Hosensack, was to become a leader in the musical life of the church.

Depending on the moods of local militia officers, other Mennonites continued to pay heavy fines for the remainder of the war. Miller Mathias Pennypacker along the Pickering Creek, having first had his mill torn up by the British and then during the Valley Forge encampment of the Americans having had his barn used as a magazine and his orchard as a parade ground, paid fifty-five pounds in 1780, with his fellow Mennonites John and David Buckwalter and Christian Halteman. The fact that the hardworking plain people were prospering while ignoring the war as much as possible continued to gall the military minded. Colonel Philip Marsteller of the "Commissary Department" complained that the "wealthy Menonists" from around Lancaster would "drive Flocks of Cattle over the Mountains in the Spring Season to the great distress of the poor Inhabitants." These cattle must be surplus riches, or they would be kept at home, "and therefore ought to be taken from them." The Colonel requested "10 or 12 men" to help round up and confiscate the animals.

Occasionally tempers flared, as when Amishman Isaac Kaufman of Berks County had been asked for his horse, and had refused indignantly, saying, "You are Rebels, and I will not give a Horse to such blood Spilling persons!" Isaac was indicted for "speaking against the publick defense of America," convicted of "misprision of Treason," and jailed in Reading, only to be pardoned when passions had cooled.

Mennonites and Brethren remained extremely reluctant to give up their loyalty to the king, even though they could not, as many other Loyalists, express their feelings violently. In Lancaster County they went so far as to draw up an "address and petition to the king" in secret, thinking that someone like Christopher Saur III could convey it to the British commander in chief. Christian Musselman apparently had a copy of the petition in his house when some "rebels" came in, and he hastily destroyed it. It had asked for guidance as to how the king would have them behave in this emergency, whether their continuing to plant crops would be considered to be aiding the rebellion, and whether their religious freedoms could be harmed as a result of the rebellion. Christopher Saur III, who was an out-and-out Tory, reported the existence of this petition to the British authorities, and said that one indication of the Mennonites' sympathies was their kindly treatment of both British and Hessian prisoners of war.

This itself became an inflamed issue as the countryside filled up with increasing numbers of captured soldiers who had to be kept somewhere, pending the outcome of the war. Already at Christmas 1778 5,000 British troops had been marched 700 miles from Massachusetts, where their government had failed to redeem them according to its agreement, to Virginia, where they could be quartered with less danger. Passing through fertile Pennsylvania, the Hessians were amazed at the unparalleled size and strength of the farmers' horses. They also "liked it best" when staying with "Quakers, Anabaptists and other sects" along the route of march. They liked the Pennsylvania countryside so well, in fact, that about 400 escaped, some to marry local girls.

Soon there were arrests of people who had allowed deserters to stay in their houses, even for only one night as unknown transients. Abraham Boehm and Jacob Whisler, with a Methodist preacher, were accused of taking cattle to the king's troops. For the next several years a string of cases kept the issue alive. Time after time citizens were sentenced to jail, fines, or whippings for acts of kindness to British prisoners on the loose, or on the way to freedom by way of a secret series of friendly homes. Authorities had become so determined to stop escapes from the Lancaster barracks that spies were placed among the prisoners. When Benjamin Bowman was hailed into court for advising a "prisoner" to go to New York, the man he thought he was aiding revealed that he had been sent by his American officer to circulate through the country as a pretended British prisoner, and find out who would do anything at all for him.

That even Whigs were not in favor of all the punishment meted out on this score was evident when four militia captains signed the petition of Mennonite Henry Martin, who had been fined for "aiding . . . British Prisoners of War to join the Enemies of the United States of America." Most of the fine was later remitted, after a further appeal by Brother Peter Miller of the Ephrata Cloister, a man whose intelligent voice was respected by the authorities, though he too was a defenseless Christian. Miller referred to Henry Martin's (and others') crime as simply not apprehending British deserters. The Pennsylvania legislators passed new laws to levy penalties for even this.

Just west of the Schuylkill in Chester County the Mennonites and Brethren were also drawn into this agitation. Jacob Longacre, a farmer along the road that ran northwest from Valley Forge, had been "often called upon for Forrage, Provisions, Quarters, Team, etc." by the American authorities, and had seen his house used as a hospital for several months after the battles of Brandywine and Germantown. With Mathias Pennypacker, the husband of his niece, Jacob had paid a considerable price for living near the line of march, though unlike the younger miller he was, at sixty-nine, past the age of militia fines. It was a common occurrence for travelers to knock at the Longacre's roadside door and ask for refreshment or lodging. One day while Jacob was many miles from home and his seventy-year-old wife, Susannah, was alone with only an eight-year-old girl for companion, several men stopped and asked for a meal. When she had set food and drink on the table, as had been her custom "for many years past," they said that they were British prisoners. Susannah, who labored under great bodily infirmity," answered their request for directions along "the Great Road" by her house to the home of a person whose name they mentioned. Perhaps it was Martin Urner, the nearby Dunkard bishop, whose farm had been ruined by foraging troops, and who now also gave the traveling prisoners food and drink, or Frederick Bosshart, neighbor of miller Pennypacker, whose farm had been laid waste by the British at the time they had vandalized Pennypacker's mill.

In any case, the "prisoners" turned out to be American spies looking for people who would help prisoners, and Susannah, Martin, and Frederick were arrested in a general crackdown. They were fined 150 pounds each, and the elderly Susannah was warned that if she defaulted she was to receive 117 lashes "on her bare back at the public Post." All three appealed for clemency, their neighbors joining in petitions which emphasized their honorable manner of life. Bishop Urner, who said he fed the travelers not "because they were British, but because they were men," begged the authorities to "act according to the Golden rule."

Such were the uncertainties of these angry years of civil strife that when Jacob Longacre wrote his will twelve years after the end of the war, assigning the farm to his son Jacob, Jr., he stipulated that in the event of another war, if the woods of these acres "should be damaged, because of giving wood to the army," the rate of valuation should be lowered. As for Deacon Christian Meyer, now approaching his eighties, he spelled out painstakingly in his will that all his legacies should be paid out in "Gold and Silver . . . a golden half Johannes weighing nine pennyweight, to be paid and received for three Pounds & a milled spanish Dollar for seven shillings and six Pence." By the time he died, five years later, money was more stable again, and the register of wills under the government Christian had not trusted was none other than Frederick Muhlenberg, son of the well-known Lutheran pastor. The Revolution, while it had ruined some people, had given political opportunity to others.

No one resented the new government more bitterly
than a family who were neighbors of Christian Meyer's
grandchildren in Bucks County. The Doanes, long a
respected name among the rural Quakers in Plumstead
Township, had sympathized with the king rather than the
Congress, been attainted of treason after the British had
left Philadelphia, and, with other outspoken Loyalists,
had their property confiscated. Their resentment knew no
bounds. In 1781, after the decisive American victory at
Yorktown, Virginia, several of the brothers left their
homes to live in caves and forests, and began to swoop
down on unsuspecting tax collectors to rob them of their
receipts, and thus take back by force what in their opinion
had been robbed from them. Time after time their Whig
enemies had sought vainly to capture them, and once
their footsteps were traced directly to the door of one of
the Meyers' homes. The Tory fugitives were actually hiding in a hollowed-out space behind the cellar wall,
covered by two large stones replaced, it was said, by
father Meyer himself. Though the pursuers came so close
to their prey that the hiding men could listen to their con-
versation, the Whigs left empty-handed. On another occasion, some time after their property had been confiscated, several of the outlaws and their horses were
concealed behind cleverly stacked hay in the barn of Abraham Wismer, with no one but Abraham aware of their
presence. Thus the Mennonite farmer who had once
carted supplies with the family horses at the demand of
the American Army now gave neighborly aid to partisans
on the other side, though he himself would join the forces
of neither.

A climax of the Doanes' Robin Hood-like career came

in November of 1781, when nine men seized 2,000 pounds in currency in a raid on the county treasury at Newtown. After they had divided their loot, two immediately made for Canada where they intended to settle, five were captured and hanged, and another who escaped in Philadelphia fled to his brothers in Canada. A year or two later still another Doane outlaw, Moses, was shot along the Tohickon Creek on the farm next to Abraham Wismer's. Abraham, husband of Christian Meyer's granddaughter Fronica, would often describe, in later life, the pathetic funeral procession of a few neighbors, two women, and a dog. As the women wept bitterly, Abraham would recall, the dog stepped to the edge of the grave and looked in mournfully.

This brought to an end the notorious raids, and later members of the defenseless Meyer and the violent Doane family would live together peacefully in the pioneer country of Ontario, once again under the king's rule which they preferred. With them would eventually be John Fretz, who had refused his gun to the American collectors, and who would be ordained the first Mennonite deacon in Canada. Braving unimaginably muddy roads and dense forests, the Meyers, Kratzes, Hochs, Hunsbergers, and others now reenacted the pioneering adventures of their grandparents, lured once again by the hope of fresh land and a reprieve from the quarrels of a people throwing off their royal authority.

All their dissatisfactions, their trials, and their taxes were minor, however, when weighed beside the unmitigated tragedy visited upon Pennsylvania's Indians in the course of the war waged by their white conquerors. After the British had left Philadelphia they incited the

Mohawks of New York to harass the Pennsylvania
frontiers from the north. Bloody atrocities were committed on both sides, and General Washington urgently demanded a final solution: the total destruction of the Indian settlements of the Six Nations. In the summer of
1779 his wish was granted, with a "glorious bonfire."
Forty Indian towns, one containing 128 houses, were put
to the torch. All corn and grain were destroyed, with
every fruit tree that could be found. It was the end of the
Six Nations, who fled to Canada. One of the officers in the
American forces who had exterminated the Indian towns
noted in his journal that the "good effects" of these "glorious achievements" would be given their due credit by
"the eloquence of time."

But it was a village of nonfighting Indians in Ohio who
would be offered as the most poignant sacrifice of all to
the insensate lusts of intestine war. At Gnadenhutten,
"The Place of Grace," Moravians had hopefully settled a
village of America's original people, converted to a quiet,
agricultural life of following Jesus, and the forsaking of all
bitterness and wrath. No longer did the white man's gun
nor their own tomahawks serve them as a means of sett-
ling human differences. Though Europeans called them
savages, they had become as defenseless, in the image of
the Lamb of God, as any Moravian or Mennonite of white
skin. But when other Indians who had been involved in
frontier assassinations stopped in their village and were
given hospitality, the enmity of the frontier white Americans was made total. Men who are determining the
ownership of territory by the gun will allow no such thing
as neutrality. Corralling ninety of the Indians (including
five who were "assistant missionaries") in their own log

buildings, rough American soldiers tomahawked them one by one—man, woman, boy, girl, and infant. Not one of the Christian Indians offered resistance. It was said that one of their number, "Abraham the Mahickon" had spent the previous night counselling them to die without revenge, as Christ on the cross. Thus were the converted savages dealt justice by being fed into the simplistic maw of the white man's war for liberty.

When at last this war was proclaimed by Congress to be at an end, on April 11, 1783, there were no celebrations among the Mennonites. In Philadelphia the occasion was marked by a general "illumination"—each house having a burning candle in the front window. Although "decorum and harmony" were "earnestly recommended . . .and a general discountenance to the least appearance of riot," gangs roamed the city smashing panes where they found no candles. But along the Skippack, Branch, Indian, Tohickon, and Neshaminy the night was unbroken. Nevertheless, the bitterness of civil schism had left there too a lasting curse so that those whose ancestors had opted out of physical wars centuries before in Europe had now conducted their own neighborhood quarrel.

Christian Funk felt vindicated in his support of the victorious American government, and expected an acknowledgment of the rightness of his views from his estranged brethren. To his dismay, as he later wrote to the public, "no minister would give me a hearing," and the stories of his sharp business dealings only flared afresh. "Christian Funk is a township thief and a congress cheat," was the public accusation. One evening the bishop went to visit his alienated neighbor minister, and challenged him: "Jacob Oberholtzer, before this, we were

good friends, and now such a bitter root has sprung up."
Listing the rumors he had heard, Christian claimed in-
nocence of them all, and awaited Jacob's response. The
minister defended each charge with details, claiming that
as to his ram, of which Christian had long ago cut off the
ears, he would be glad to bring it forth as evidence on demand.

"Jacob," implored Mrs. Oberholtzer, "do be still about
that ram!"

"You have cheated the township out of twenty-five
pounds," persisted Jacob, "and I can prove it to you."

Henry Landis, a sympathetic neighbor brought along
by Christian for support, interjected, "Why, Jacob, you
wouldn't say, would you, that Funk out-and-out cheated
the township, but rather that the township was cheated
by his horse?"

"No," insisted the minister, "he cheated it."

Although Christian dismissed the charges as baseless,
Oberholtzer stated flatly that "he would prove them
every day" with ten witnesses. The impasse remained
fixed, and there was to be no resolution short of Christian's rescinding his well-known partisan views. Though
the war itself was now history, Christian's very preoccu-
pation with political issues was, as the brethren saw it, a
symptom of a "worldly" spirit that could not long be
contained within their traditional way of life. In return,
Christian observed a year after the war's ending that
some of his "opponents" seemed still to be uneasy, feeling that the peace established by the treaty with England
was not real, and arguing "that if congress is a government, they and their ministers have been in an error these
seven years." Hoping for a sympathetic hearing, Chris-

tian's son-in-law John Detweiler, now a Funkite minister, signed a challenge to the main body of Mennonites to disclaim Jacob Oberholtzer's charges. If they did not, the Funkites threatened, the charges would be published openly so that the world could judge their falseness.

By now Philadelphia County had been divided, and the northern section named Montgomery. Other unprecedented changes came forth rapidly as both federal and state governments reorganized and levied taxes which at first struck many people as unwarranted. There was dissension. "What will come of it only God knows," wrote immigrant Deacon Rudolph Landes of Deep Run. "Many inhabitants of Pennsylvania cannot become reconciled" to the taxes. But while others may foment "little warfares" over these "demands for money," observes the deacon, the followers of Christ will peacefully "give unto the king whatever belongs to the king, and to God what is His," and love their enemies so that, as Christ said, "You may be the children of your Father in heaven."

Though he was not in sympathy with the Funkite faction, Deacon Landes was here clearly identifying the legitimate public authority with Congress, then barely able to muster a quorum for meeting in Philadelphia, and its new Constitution still unfinished. Since Rudolph's acceptance of the new government's standing is clearly and matter of factly declared, a modern observer may surmise that Christian Funk's alienation was sustained less by genuine political differences than by pettier grudges, and a different rate of speed in relating to new developments. For even after both factions willingly acknowledged the new government, their separation remained unbridged.

As the new century brought younger bishops to the
scene, Christian Funk tested their willingness to vindi-
cate him, and reinstate him in his office. Though they
once again took up the task of reconciliation, observing
that it would bring great pleasure to the various congregations, and Christian and his accuser Jacob
Oberholtzer actually reached the point of greeting each
other with the kiss of peace, agreement broke down over
whether in allowing himself to be reinstated, Christian
would be implying that those who had joined his group,
including many who had died, had all been in the wrong.
There was prayer, with the ministers kneeling together,
vote taking, and discussion in the semiannual conference
at Franconia (Indianfield). Should the ministers whom
Christian had independently ordained be allowed to
continue in their offices once Christian had been reac-
cepted? Would the rumors of his sharp business practices
be pronounced to have been completely false? All this became irrelevant, unhappily, when it became apparent
that the Indianfield congregation would not accept Christian Funk back even if their ministers would.

By now the aged bishop was living ten miles from Indianfield, and he was still clinging to the hope of vindica-
tion. In his eightieth year he wrote another argumentive
pamphlet on behalf of his "defenseless evangelical congregation." Two years later he died unreconciled,
fourteen years after the passing of his fellow-bishop
Andrew Ziegler. Christian's followers, now including
grandchildren of his opponents Henry Rosenberger and
Christian Meyer, then built four small meetinghouses.
For a decade or two their fellowship survived, agonizing
over questions of intermarriage with the larger group of

Mennonites, until a visiting preacher of a dissident group in Lancaster County, John Herr, gathered their remnants into a tiny new denomination, "the Reformed Mennonites."

Thus faded at last the bitterness of a division that, on the world scene, had created a vast new nation—a constitutional, unkinged republic—and in isolated Indian Creek valley, ripped asunder the tight-woven fabric of a Mennonite community.

As the 200th anniversary of the birth of their new nation and of their own family schism approached, Indianfield seemed at last to be merging with a spreading greater Philadelphia. The latest Funk's Mill was an art gallery, Christian Meyer's house had made way for a turnpike that also roared by Henry Rosenberger's barn, and John Bergey's acres were strolled by casual suburban golfers. Only Jacob Oberholtzer's quiet creek-side farm lay substantially unchanged by progress.

Now the descendants of these defenseless but quarrelsome Christians, stirred by their own troubled times to reexamine fundamental questions of identity and loyalty, searched attics and chests to reconstruct the story of the intertwining of the split at Indian Creek with the vast one that gave their nation its birth. Among the papers assembled at the Bicentennial appeared an 1804 ciphering book of thirteen-year-old Abraham Wismer, namesake son of the Revolutionary carter from Deep Run who had married Deacon Christian Meyer's granddaughter Fronica. In it we may observe the Mennonite pupil struggling to acquaint himself with the language in which his descendants would think and speak, now that the destiny of North America was settled. In the awkward spelling of the boy who would one day, like his great-grandfather Meyer, serve as a deacon among the defenseless Pennsylvania Dutch Mennonites, is preserved a testimony to the sometimes irreconcilable loyalties that in his father's day had torn colony from king, and split the seams of his covenant fellowship:

> *Abraham Wismer is my name*
> *and Geromany is my nation*
> *Amarica is my Dwelling place*
> *and Christ is my Salvation.*

An Author's Fantasy

In the delicious peace of a summer Sunday evening I strolled among the gravestones of the Colonial Mennonites of Lower Salford. Though the mossy markers themselves remained, much about the scene had altered decisively since they were first set in the recently cleared soil nearly two centuries earlier. The homestead of Heinrich Ruth, from which these gentle slopes had been cut out, had long ago lost all trace of its log cabin, rail fences, and springhouse, though a lilac by a tiny brook revealed where the pioneer had planted his earthly *Wohnung*. The meetinghouse, still simple in outline, had swollen to an immense expanse of brick. And a bell-crowned schoolhouse, though empty of children now for a generation, called to mind the beloved schoolteacher Christopher Dock, who here taught reading, writing, reckoning, singing, and faith. Having lived far longer than his expectations, he nevertheless had never dreamed, by 1771, of a "United States of America."

The graveyard itself had lost its wall as it grew up the slope, and, as the lawn mower made its debut, suffered the indignity of having its stones rearranged in rows of military precision so that the grass might be frequently and smoothly clipped. Thus, I mused, do we line up the symbols of our past to fit the tastes of our times.

Before one simple stone I paused and pondered just such an anomaly. Under its small arched top was carved the name of Joseph Alderfer, farmer across the rise from the meetinghouse in the time of the American Revolution, member of this congregation of defenseless Christians, and brother of the builder of the house where I was born. Before his stone drooped a fresh banner—the red, white, and blue of Joseph Alderfer's earthly country and mine. It is a country I love.

Nevertheless I stooped, withdrew the flag, and respectfully laid it on the grass.

"Why did you do that?" It was the surprised voice of my neighbor, an elderly, good-hearted cousin who also carried the Alderfer name.

I did it, Jacob, not in disdain for our country, but because this flag was mistakenly planted. It was one of thousands placed on Memorial Day in honor of men who two centuries earlier had taken up arms to defend the liberty of rebelling American Colonies against the authority of the king of England. Both sides claimed divine rights, but in fact John had not, as most of the other men whose neighboring graves are similarly decorated had not, fought in that war. He had not wished the war to be declared, and he regretted, at first, that it turned out as it did. His father, born a Lutheran near the Rhine, after migration to Pennsylvania had married his Mennonite employer's widow, espousing with her the defenseless creed of her people. Joseph, too, had married the Mennonite granddaughter of Deacon Christian Meyer, and his brother John had taken Elizabeth Rosenberger, whose parents had brought with them a Bible of their Swiss ancestors, now nearly two centuries old, inscribed on the flyleaves with Mennonite teachings. For Joseph and his brothers, who accepted these teachings, all killing had now been abandoned, and they paid heavy fines to his militia officers rather than participate in their war.

Then why was Joseph's grave marked with the banner of a grateful nation?

Such was the rage for national pedigree, half a century ago, that sonorous genealogists reassured family reunions en masse that such and such an ancestor had been "a soldier in the Revolution." From the rosters of countless militia companies were assiduously copied the names of farmers and artisans so that their descendants might honor them, and thereby claim the right to be enrolled as Sons and Daughters of the American Revolution

On those lists was the name of Joseph Alderfer, along with that of every other man in the community between eighteen and fifty-three. But neither he nor his Mennonite and Brethren friends may be designated, in the hitherto accepted sense, American patriots. For them, the Revolution seemed a tragic adventure in human impatience. It was in respect for truth, then, that I had gently laid aside the flag.

Joseph's relatives living inconspicuously along the Branch Creek in the nearby valley, never understood much of the world's to-do that rumbled so importantly at the edges of their quiet, agricultural existence. For a century and a half they lived as separately as the world would allow. When patriots came to plant commemorative flags before their graves, the shy farmers assumed that such impressive strangers must surely, in their purposeful gestures, know what they were about.

What is to be made of so stubbornly quiet, so exasperatingly withdrawn a people, who would gladly have ignored, had that been possible, the war that gave them the country they and their children have ever since enjoyed? What shall we think of people who would refuse to raise a gun toward a fellow human, even if he were an enemy, but then could not refrain from bickering among themselves and dividing their church?

Surely, at least, we have come far enough in our modern maturity that we need no longer make of them something they were not, only to entertain ourselves with notions of an authentic American pedigree. Surely their bones should be allowed to rest unratified by the symbol of a Revolution they regretted and even helped to hinder. Surely their withdrawal may be granted whatever integrity it had, as it continues to question the identification of the career of a human being, in the final perspective of death, with his participation in this or that episode of civil strife. As if we indeed wished to face the tribunal of eternity with the claim, "When the fife piped and the drum rattled in my corner of God's creation, I followed the colors!"

Who, I wondered, is to be a spokesman for these inarticulate, sheepish farmers, these "Dutch Menonists" mocked by Dr. Benjamin Rush as the Germans among whom "ignorance" was most prevalent in Pennsylvania? When that stylish Philadelphia physician had wished to galvanize the minds of his fellow citizens for a cause he considered supremely important—independence from Great Britain—he had found and stimulated the fiery pen of a Paine, and thereby won an ambivalent populace to the cause. That cause, not without its moral ambiguities and respected opponents, had suddenly acquired from the passion of the propagandist a sweet, intense simplicity, a "common sense" that appealed directly to the universal heart of a latent "America." To be an American patriot then seemed the call of nature and religion.

But what of the claims of a realm that obstinately recognizes the validity of no wars, that accepts as its own long-accomplished Revolution the coming of a Prince of Peace in ancient Palestine? What of the agricultural Germans whose heads subscribed to another kind of common sense: that war for any reason is beneath the dignity of beings in the image of God, and has been obsolete, nay, forbidden, for 1,700 odd years? What of people who will give their own lives before taking those of their enemies?

Is there no equally eloquent pamphleteer, no advocate to fling out boldly into the public forum the imagery of such a dream? Is there no irresistible tide of yearning in the soul of a potential United Hearts of Humankind that will bear up the passionate orator's emotions and sweep from his lips in orotund tones the message that it is not killing but seeding time?

Meditating thus among the tombstones of these rustic noncooperators in the birth of their earthly nation, I wondered how I might offer my own small voice on behalf of this hitherto unpopular cause. But would I not be too prone, I mused, to extenuate out of love the inconsistencies of my defenseless ancestors; too much their son to recognize that their troubles in the Revolutionizing society of 1776 were not unique to them; too appreciative, even, of the American Constitution, to countenance fully the parochial views of a people who could not recognize the advent of a benevolent ideal?

In spite of such questionings, I could not dismiss a persistent fantasy, there in the graveyard twilight, of a ghostly orator, clad in long colonial coat and breeches, rising from among these stones to harangue the surrounding maples with a flood of peaceful, antique eloquence. It was as though each leaf represented a fascinated human face in a murmurous multitude. Here in my dream, where no pompous official intimidated nor any wise academic frowned, I sensed I would at last hear a new kind of message. I was not disappointed. I began to hear the golden, heaving passion of the orator's voice, as its music floated across the valley and out toward the wide world. Though the words seemed indistinct, its burden was that of the human heart, the conscious groaning of creation for peace on earth. Straining vainly to understand the words, I seemed to find placed in my hands a spectral pamphlet, on whose pages the words of the oration seemed to glow momentarily before they evanesced:

Take away from among these stones the prideful flags of nations, for this is holy ground. Call them not Americans, though their offspring have rejoiced in that name. Call them pilgrims, who chose rather the reproach of the Prince of Peace than to enjoy the pleasures of citizenship for a season, so that they might in all due obedience honor the most high God and bless their fellows.

In their narrow hearts the love of God was shed abroad so that it kept their calloused hands on the plow when their neighbors' grasped the sword. They could not leave home for the fray: 'twas seeding time. To plant, not to destroy, was their calling. To be helpful to all and hurtful to none was their Christly creed. Were they not then patriots of the human race? And more, were they not revolutionaries? Was not their slowness, nay, their refusal to address their differences with sword and rifle—was not this an adumbration of what must one day be the heritage of humankind? Was not their patience at least as new, as revolutionary, as the ancient recourse to blood-letting? Have ye truly de-

termined, ye medallioned generals and ye opposing revolutionaries, that the good can arrive among us only if we first
spend a season of killing each other? That without the
tumult of the Revolution ye wrought, there could have been
no resolution, no evolution, without the lust and rapine of
war? Is it thus ye establish the national borders ye then
claim as the gift of heaven?

Have ye indeed seen, in your stern pragmatisms, farther
into reality than these clumsy farmers? Would ye have had
them leave their way of humble peace to join in the bloody
revolutions of their lifetime so that, rather than citizens of
eternity, they might have been American patriots? And ye
solemn theologians, who have found reasons, even since
your "Reformation," for Christ's followers to defend their
countries' flags in blood through moaning centuries—is it
yet your claim that this too is where God's unfolding salvation works: in the clash of ever newly invented arms?

Ye geniuses who now soar to the moon, whence ye view
the earth in its marbled blue beauty, yea, who rain probing
rockets on Mars—can ye not explore the Mars in the soul of
humankind, and turn those spiky wastes into fields of
peace? Is not God's salvation as nigh us as our hearts and
mouths, if we would but believe and confess?

A sudden hush fell upon the maples, and I feared that
the mellifluously welcome oration of my dream was at an
end. But as I clutched the antique pamphlet, I found, to
my great joy, that there was more:

Is it not still seeding time, my brothers and sisters, when
the real crop of the love of God must be planted in the
human soul, rather than the dragon's teeth of war that only
yield more sworded soldiers? Can not the testimony of these
simple, stubborn farmers fall as seed on the hearts of the
world? Can we not finally turn away, like them, from the
wars by which great and excellent men, having gravely
pondered, decide that our difficulties with our foreign

neighbors must be settled? They have had their say, have
they not? These admirable Franklins and Rittenhouses,
these Tamerlanes and Talleyrands, these heroic Bolivars and
iron Bismarcks, these cunning Kissingers and Kosygins—for
all recorded history. The stage has been theirs, the devotion
of the historian, the scrutiny of the archivists they hire to
perpetuate the rumor of their vast deeds. But, while the
blood-soaked earth continues to groan exquisitely in Ireland,
Angola, Rhodesia, Lebanon for a new harvest of peace, is it
not at long last seeding time, when other, less dangerous
heroes may be hailed?

Think ye, my fellow humans, that we shall be instructed
in this longed for harvest by the wise and prudent of the
earth? The poets and painters? Think ye that the
descendants of these farmers who left their fathers' peaceful
ways—Indian-killing Custer, draftmaster Hershey, or
Europe-conquering Eisenhower—having gained the
worldly wisdom and glory of their day, can instruct us in
their forebears' defenseless teachings? Will they not rather
lead us, with their grim assessment of "necessity" ratified
by the current crop of professors and philosophers, back
down that ancient, gory track?

O ye who love mankind, who are your true heroes, your
patriots? Are they still those who ride statuesquely before
you to Homeric slaughters? Those whose fantastic brains
have built for you an unbelievable bomb?

I was jolted from my dream as this final dark word
seemed to leap from the yellowed page and burst in the
somber sunset radiance at the western end of the Branch
Valley. My hand was empty, and the mellow voice had
given way to peaceful crickets. In regret, I attempted to
complete the thrilling oration myself, as I glanced at the
multitudinous leaves, my only auditors:

Think momentarily, my friends, after 200 years, of an

unlettered remnant of defenseless Christians, dwelling in
the crevices of Penn's Woods. Here, while the world turned
the gun they had invented into the ancient service of war, a
Bucks County Quaker whittled out and invented the mold-
board plow in the jail where he had been placed as a non-
cooperator, to while away the world's killing-time. And soon
thereafter, a Mennonite farmer in Lancaster County
fashioned a grain-cradle, followed, many years later, by
another who devised an automatic baler. It was seeding
time! and still is, though now the baler works have been
bought by Sperry-Rand, who made the sight to aim the
bomb toward our mother earth. . . .

Sensing my inability to maintain the eloquence of the
departed orator, I betook myself somewhat soberly to my
nearby home. Was not my twilight vision, I wondered,
largely a projection of filial piety? Was it not the all too
common veneration of our ancestors, however humble,
whereby we attempt to purchase for ourselves reflected
significance?

And yet the fervent pathos of that echoing voice among
the tombstones, yearning out across the valley toward
Philadelphia and the world beyond—the logic of my
dream—stunned me in a sense of reality more convincing
than that of the headlines of the newspaper sprawled on
my desk. "Informed sources in strife-torn Belfast," began
the report, but my eyes drifted away in a surfeit of the familiar, dreary tale of civil agony. It is not news. It is the
immemorial repetition of what humans have nearly always done when their collective wills have clashed. It
would be news if they at long last, like the defenseless
farmers of Penn's Woods, found war itself to be worse
than the evils it was meant to avoid. Would that not be a
revolution to crown revolutions?

Who, in the Memorial Days of such a consummation, would be honored as its pioneers? Who would be seen as the prototypes of the new society that Marx, having despaired of the reality of Christ, secularly substituted, or of the new man that Mao wished for? Who but such as these farmers and weavers, simply obedient to the Sermon on the Mount, unskilled in the sophistry by which learned humans of all races and ideologies justify or accept their hellish wars?

Startled at the audacity of my thoughts, I let my eyes stray from the newspaper to a little pamphlet lying beside it, and there read even more daring words, from the pen of none other than the erudite Dr. Benjamin Rush. They had been written, apparently, long after he had instigated Thomas Paine to compose his incandescent *Common Sense*, and after the passion of Revolution had cooled. As I read, I concluded in amazement that the doctor, too, must have heard my ghostly orator, for his utterance here was a guarded but eloquent hope regarding the defenseless Christians whose "ignorance" he had been wont to chide:

> Perhaps those German sects of Christians who refuse to bear arms for the shedding of human blood may be preserved by Divine Providence as the center of a circle which shall gradually embrace all nations of the Earth in a perpetual treaty of friendship and peace.

God grant, Dr. Rush, that your dream of such a revolution may be fulfilled, and that its rosters may be overwhelmingly inscribed, beneath the brief lists of these defenseless Christians, with ever increasing multitudes of new names.

A Note on Sources

Basic to my research were the considerable manuscript materials selected by Robert F. Ulle from the holdings of the Historical Society of Pennsylvania in Philadelphia. Much of this material, as well as much more that is not drawn upon for my narrative, will appear in edited form in the forthcoming "source book" on Mennonite experience in the Revolution edited by Richard K. MacMaster, Samuel Horst, and Robert F. Ulle. This will be the basic reference tool in this field. A valuable preview of this material has appeared in Richard MacMaster's Christian Obedience in Revolutionary Times (see below). A formal history of the role of the peace churches in the Colonial era is also being prepared by Donald Durnbaugh.

I will not list in detail the family histories and genealogies which I perused, except to mention some of the Mennonite names for which there exist such records available in libraries at the Christopher Dock High School, Lansdale, Pennsylvania; the Historical Society of Pennsylvania (the most complete collection); or the Mennonite Historical Library at Goshen, Indiana: Ackerman, Alderfer, Beidler, Bergey, Borneman, Bowman, Cassel, Clemens, Clemmer, Delp, Freed, Fretz, Funk, Godshalk, Hagey, Kolb, Kratz, Latshaw, Longacre, Moyer, Rosenberger, Ruth, Oberholtzer, Stauffer, Souder, and Wismer.

Omitting such obvious items as general county histories, I have listed here a sampling of some of the important sources from which I have obtained information:

Allebach, David K. *History of Hatfield, Montgomery County, Pennsylvania.* Reprinted 1975 by Hatfield Community Bicentennial Commission.

Bender, Wilbur, J. "Pacifism Among the Mennonites, Amish Mennonites and Schwenkfelders of Pennsylvania to 1783, " *Mennonite Quarterly Review,* I (1927), 23-40.

Brock, Peter C. *Pacifism in the United States From the Colonial Era to the First World War.* Princeton: Princeton University Press, 1968.

Brunk, Gerald R. and James O. Lehman. *A Guide to Select Revolutionary Records Pertaining to Mennonites and Other Pacifist Groups in Southeastern Pennsylvania and Maryland 1775-1800.* Harrisonburg, Va.: Eastern Mennonite College, 1974. (See "Kraybill," below.)

Brunk, Harry Anthony. *History of Mennonites in Virginia 1727-1900,* Vol. I. Harrisonburg, Va.: H. A. Brunk, 1959.

Claussen, W. Edmunds. *Revolutionary War Years in Berks, Chester and Montgomery Counties, Pennsylvania.* Boyertown, Pa.: W. E. Claussen, 1973.

Commager, Henry Steele and Richard B. Morris (eds.). *The Spirit of Seventy-Six: The Story of the American Revolution as Told by Participants,* Vol. I. Indianapolis: Bobbs-Merrill Company, Inc., 1958.

Dambly, Whitman P. "Washington's Headquarters at Skippack," *Bulletin of the Montgomery County Historical Society,* II (1940).

Derstine, Kenton. "The Nonresistance of the Mennonites in Southeastern Pennsylvania During the Revolutionary War." Unpublished History Seminar Paper at Eastern Mennonite College, Harrisonburg, Va., February, 1972.

Durnbaugh, Donald F. *The Brethren in Colonial America.* Elgin, Ill.: The Brethren Press, 1967.

From Brandywine Through the Perkiomen Valley to Valley

Forge September and October 1777, Vol. 5, No. 4 (October 1927) of *The Perkiomen Region*, Pennsburg, Pa. A forty-six page compilation of excerpts from diaries, orderly books, letters, etc.

Funk, Christian. *A Mirror for All Mankind*. Norristown, Pa.: J. Winnard, 1814. Reprinted in *Mennonite Historical Bulletin*, XXXV (January 1974), 3-11.

Hamilton, J. Taylor and Kenneth G. Hamilton. *History of the Moravian Church*. Bethlehem, Pa.: Interprovincial Board of Christian Education Moravian Church in America, 1967.

Heckler, James Y. *The History of Harleysville and Lower Salford Township*. Harleysville, Pa.: Harleysville *News*, 1886.

Hershberger, Guy Franklin, *War, Peace, and Nonresistance* Scottdale, Pa.: Herald Press, 1944.

Kauffman, S. Duane. "Religious Pacifists and the American Revolution." Unpublished "unit" of "Selected Readings and Suggested Student Activities," Revised September 1, 1975. Fourteen "case-studies," compiled for use in Mennonite High Schools.

Kessler, Charles H. *Lancaster in the Revolution*. Lititz, Pa.: Sutter House, 1975.

Kraybill, Mary Jean, Gerald R. Brunk, and James O. Lehman. *A Guide to Select Revolutionary War Records Pertaining to Mennonites and Other Pacifist Groups in Southeastern Pennsylvania and Maryland 1775-1800. Number Two*. Harrisonburg, Va.: Eastern Mennonite College, 1974. (See Brunk, Gerald, above.)

Kratz, Henry W. "Washington at Pennebecker's Mills," *Historical Society of Montgomery County Sketches*, II (1900).

Landes, Henry S. *History of Souderton*. Souderton, Pa.: The Souderton *Independent*, 1930.

Lehman, James O. "The Mennonites of Maryland During the Revolutionary War" *Mennonite Quarterly Review*, (July 1976), 200-229.

MacMaster, Richard K. *Christian Obedience in Revolutionary Times: The Peace Churches and the American Revolution*. Akron, Pa.: Mennonite Central Committee, 1976.

Matthews, Edward. *A History of Towamencin Township*. Skippack, Pa.: Skippack Press, 1880.

Mennonite Encyclopedia, 4 vols.

Montgomery, Morton, L. *History of Berks County, Pennsylvania, in the Revolution*, from 1774 to 1783. Reading, Pa., 1894, reprinted by the Historical Society of Berks County, 1975.

Moore, Frank (compiler). *The Diary of the American Revolution 1775-1781*. Abridged, edited, and with an Introduction by John Anthony Scott. New York: Washington Square Press, 1967.

Muhlenberg, Henry Melchior. *The Journals of Henry Melchior Muhlenberg*, 3 vols. Ed. Theodore G. Tappert and John W. Doberstein. Muhlenberg Press, 1942-48.

Pennsylvania Archives, First, Second, and Third Series. This many-volumed series reproduces colonial and Revolutionary records such as tax-lists, militia rosters, and correspondence. Though it must be used with care, it is an indispensable source.

Pennypacker, Samuel Whitaker. *Annals of Phoenixville and its Vicinity*. Philadelphia, 1873.

Posen, Thomas A. "Washington Along the Skippack," *Bulletin of the Historical Society of Montgomery County*, XIX (Fall 1974), 230-248.

Roach, Hannah Benner. "The Pennsylvania Militia in 1777," *Pennsylvania Genealogical Magazine*, XXIII (1964), 161-229.

Smith, C. Henry. *The Mennonite Immigration to Pennsylvania in the Eighteenth Century*. Norristown, Pa.: The Norristown Press, 1929. Contains valuable material but must be used with discretion.

Schwenkfelder Library, Pennsburg, Pa. A miscellany of material pertaining to the area of the Franconia Mennonites, combining information from printed and oral sources.

Specht, J. Henry. *A History of Towamencin Township*. Kulpsville, Pa.: Kulpsville Lions Club, n.d.

Stevens, Sylvester K. *Pennsylvania: Birthplace of a Nation*.

New York: Random House, 1964.

Stoudt, John Baer. *The Life and Times of Col. John Siegfried.* Northampton, Pa.: The Cement News Print, 1914.

Stoudt, John Joseph. *Ordeal at Valley Forge: A Day-by-Day Chronicle.* Philadelphia: University of Pennsylvania Press, 1963.

Ulle, Robert F. (Compiler and Editor). "Preparing for Revolution," *Mennonite Historical Bulletin,* XXXV (July 1974), 2-7.

Wallace, Willard M. *Appeal to Arms: A Military History of the American Revolution.* New York: Harper & Brothers Publishers, 1951.

Washington, George. *The Writings of George Washington,* ed. John C. Fitzpatrick. Washington, D.C.: U.S. Government Printing Office, 1933. Vol. IX.

Weaver, Martin G. *Mennonites of Lancaster Conference.* Scottdale, Pa.: Mennonite Publishing House, 1931.

Wenger, John C. *History of the Mennonites of the Franconia Conference.* Telford, Pa.: Franconia Mennonite Historical Society, 1937.

Wright, Esmond (ed.). *Causes and Consequences of the American Revolution.* Chicago: Quadrangle Books, 1966.

Index